WHAT'S YOUR

PLAN BE?

NAME IT. CLAIM IT. LIVE IT.

BY LIBBY SPEARS

LET'S GET TOGETHER YEAH! YEAH! YEAH!

(we could have a real good time!)

I want to connect with you beyond the pages of this book.
Here is where I am hanging out.

www.facebook.com/bravocc

www.bravocc.com

www.youtube.com/libbyspears

www.slideshare.net/bravocc

I love you,
I love you,
I love you,
Thank you.

For my three biggest cheerleaders
MARK, MADDIE & TRINITY

For those teachers that took a special
interest in my education and tolerated my big mouth,
my sometimes sassy attitude, and loved me nonetheless.

WHY A SECOND EDITION?

Sometimes I think I must have been born under a lucky star. Every day I get to do the thing I love: Teach. I meet the most interesting people and help them be more successful in their endeavors. I know I am but one piece of the puzzle. There are many other people working just as hard at what they do to complete the success equation for my clients, but I gotta tell ya: I really like my piece of that puzzle.

You hear people say you have found the right job if you would do it for free. The way I try to conceptualize this idea is, "What makes you high?" The thing that makes me high is teaching a group of people, sharing stories, gleaning insights, and leaving the room better for the time we spent together.

Right now, as I type away on my Macbook, I am sitting in the busy, bustling lobby of the Marriott on Michigan Avenue and Rush Street in Chicago, Illinois. It is chilly outside, but the sun is shining, and tomorrow and the following day I will teach an accountability workshop to a group who I have become very fond of. I wouldn't trade this moment for anyone else's moment.

When I wrote the first edition of "What's Your Plan Be?" three years ago, I was motivated to get the words down on paper because in my industry there is a lot of pressure to be a "published author." I enjoyed the process of writing the book, but in retrospect, I see where the content needed a little TLC.

Six months ago I was about sixty pages into my second book when I made the decision to put the new book on the back burner and return to this book and do some of the necessary revisions to tighten up the content. As I am sure you can imagine, over three years I have added a lot of new and exciting experiences with clients, and through the rewriting process I have incorporated many of these stories. I think you will find that the second version of WYPB is a cleaner and more sophisticated version of the original. It has evolved. So have I.

I hope you enjoy the second edition and I would love your feedback! Feel free to share your thoughts with me when you are done, and if you run into my mom or dad at the grocery store, tell them I did a good job would ya?

Libby Spears

Table of Contents

There came a time when the risk to
remain tight in the bud was
more painful than the risk it took to
blossom.

Anaïs Nin

MEET WHAT'S YOUR PLAN BE?

Timing is everything right?

A recent trip to Chicago to work with a new client found me there on the same weekend as: 1. The Notre Dame versus University of Miami football game. 2. Graph Expo, one of the largest trade shows in the United States and 3. A little event called the Chicago Marathon that attracted anywhere from thirty to forty thousand people to the heart of downtown Chicago. We were all there at one time walking up and down Michigan Avenue and it's connected side streets. Miracle Mile indeed.

I decided to stay for the weekend because Chicago is one of my favorite cities to both eat in and explore. As luck would have it, my husband was working in Chicago that weekend too, and it was a great chance to work + play--one of my favorite combinations (next to peanut butter + chocolate = heaven). That Saturday I had the day to myself as my husband was working, so I made my way out onto the bustling streets in search of adventure.

My first stop would be the Art Institute of Chicago, one of the best museums in the world, and a spot I had not been to in some fifteen years. I had on my comfortable and practical footwear (Yet still fashionable. Let's get that straight. I have an image to maintain!), and set off for what I was sure would be a fantastic day in this vibrant and fast-paced city.

As it turns out, about a gabillion (100 x a trillion) people had similar plans to go out and seek their own adventures and the sidewalks and streets were littered with busy and "hurry up and get there" tourists like myself. We were all trying to get from our point A to our point B, and at times, our destinations intersected, causing stress and congestion. I am not very patient or understanding when it comes to not knowing where you are going. Even in a situation where I am a tourist, I try to behave and look like a local as much as I can, because what's worse than looking like a tourist right?

We were all little ants marching, as Dave Matthews sang so many years ago. I reminded myself, as I often must, to enjoy the journey as much as the destination. My impatience and tendency to get irritated by stupid little things is in a constant battle with the "enjoy the journey" voice in my head. Which voice do I listen to?

Because that is ultimately the question for each and every one of us. We know intellectually that the journey matters, but in the real-time, day-to-day, hustle and bustle world we live in, the journey often gets obscured, overlooked, and even abandoned. "I will pencil in 'enjoy the journey' on this fancy calendar here for hmmmmm....looks like I have an open spot on June 14th of 2000 and never."

Are you enjoying the journey?

Many times we are so focused on the end point that we fail to stop and consider if the end point is where we really want to go in the first place. This fact plays out in our conversations, choices, relationships, and decision making strategies. I am not different from you or anyone else. I lay in bed at night and play the "what if" game all the time. There are one thousand plus strategies available to me and directions from which to choose. But what direction do I go in? How do I choose a path that allows me to enjoy the journey? That is the direction I am interested in.

A little backstory...

When Bravo cc, my business adventure, was born in 2006, I knew I needed to have a catch phrase or slogan to help people remember me (Just do it!, Coke and a Smile, Where's the Beef?). At that point I understood that my handful of paying client projects had hired me because they were losing contracts when they could not close the deal with a presentation. Reaching out to me was a cry for help, and an acknowledgment on their part that something dramatic would have to change if they wanted to stand out from their competition and close deals.

I was their Plan B.

My first business card said "When it's time for Plan B," which I thought was very clever. My clients needed me to help them retool, re-imagine, and reconsider their public speaking skills so they could be more successful. Hiring me then was the recognition that Plan A--do what everyone else is doing and hope we get lucky this time around--did not work. They were ready for Plan B. For three years this catch phrase resonated and provided numerous marketing possibilities for how I told my story as a business owner. I created my marketing materials around "When it's time for Plan B" and focused workshop material around the idea. Your presentations are tired and boring? It's time for Plan B! Your team is not functioning properly? Well you need to consider Plan B. You want to move up in the organization but feel stuck? You need a Plan B. You get the picture.

But the name of this book is "When it's time for Plan Be" so clearly somewhere along the way there was a shift in my thinking. Granted, this is not Marie Curie in her laboratory finding the vaccination for polio, but I do think the story behind when I moved from Plan B to Plan BE is an interesting one. I won't keep you waiting.

Cue Jill Personius.

Jill Personius is first and foremost my friend. She is older and wiser than me, and I often joke that she is my Jimminy Cricket. To give you a visual, Jill and I look like Mutt and Jeff when we are together. I am 5'10 and Jill is about 5'3, and she looks like a ten-year-old kid. We meet regularly for coffee and talk about life, our personal and professional challenges, and we both enjoy just catching up. I am a corporate educator. Jill is a life coach. You can imagine we have some interesting conversations. Take for example, the professional Jill worked with who was transitioning out of "work life" and looking for her next chapter. She revealed to Jill she harbored a life long dream of pursuing a passion she has never shared with anyone before.

PLAN A BELIEVES THAT THE NUMBER OF HOURS WORKED = YOUR COMMITMENT TO YOUR JOB.

"Well tell me then," Jill prompted her client.

"I want to join the circus."

When Jill told me this story my immediate reaction was "Join the circus? That's crazy." But after talking about it, Jill told me there are classes available to people like her client who want to fly on a trapeze, juggle, be a clown, or have an encounter with a ferocious lion. Jill advised her client that a life in the circus might not be a possibility, but she certainly could pursue her interest in being a circus performer. So together they Googled a few key term searches and started looking for a class near her where she could live out this dream.

Stories like this are plentiful in our line of work. Every day we work with professionals, teams, and organizations who want us to help them find solutions to challenges. In 2009 over a hot cup of coffee, I found myself saying to Jill "the question is not what is your Plan B, the real question is who do you want to Be? If more people took the time to answer this question, they might not even need a Plan B in the first place."

I hear "Plan B" talk all the time! On T.V., in articles, online, in line listening to women with college-aged kids comparing their kids "back up plan" if things don't work out to their friends "back up plan." In fact, just this past weekend my neighbor revealed to me that her son was pursuing a lifelong dream to be a professional hockey referee. He went to college though, and got a degree in marketing as a back of plan of course!

The potential of my statement to Jill, "What's Your Plan Be?", did not take root until later that night when I was laying in bed mulling over the days events like a hamster running on the wheel in it's cage. I knew there was something to the idea of "Plan Be" and the following day I began to explore the possibilities. I did not want to continue to be a back-up plan for my clients. I was certain if I could challenge my clients to think differently about their success story, and how they planned out where they were headed from a new perspective that the "oh holy &*^%$ what we are doing is not working, now it is time to figure out a back up plan" would be a thing of the past.

Plan Be challenges us to face reality.

Plan Be is a new way of thinking about who you are and what you do. My take is this: Plan A was set/determined/written by someone else. Plan A sets itself up as the "right way to do things." As if there was a right way to do anything! We live in a moment in history where things are changing rapidly, thanks to the development and evolution of technology, media, travel, and the modern lifestyle. We have SO many choices, and ironically these choices are actually making our lives **more** complicated and confusing than ever before.

Unfortunately, Plan A can take a while to catch up to these changes (just ask Kodak). Plan A gets stuck in a past generation and holds steadfastly to an outdated way of doing things. Let me give you a few of the Plan A modes of thinking that I am up against all of the time when working with a client:

Plan A: This is how we have always done things
Plan B: Well that didn't work out, what's our back up plan?
Plan Be: Take the time to chart a course for success using your own set of rules and you won't need a back up plan!

1. 9 to 5 still makes sense.

2. People at the top of the food chain have figured it all out and don't need training and development.

3. Mission statements and employee handbooks make sense.

4. Annual performance reviews are effective.

5. All employees really care about is money, so that is the best way to motivate them.

6. The best decisions come from the top of the food chain.

7. We can't trust our employees.

8. The liability of firing a bad employee is just too great, so we will keep sub-par performers.

9. The smart people are the ones who have college degrees.

10. When times get bad, cut training and development first.

This list only skims the surface of the deeply entrenched modes of thinking residing in small, medium, and large organizations today.

Does the following sound familiar?

"Let's keep all the important information about where we are headed as an organization at the top to ourselves. People down the food chain don't really need to know those things to do their job."

WHAT WAS/IS THE "PLAN A" LANGUAGE FOR YOUR GENERATION?

Learn more about Generational Differences at www.slideshare.net/bravocc

"They should just be happy they have a job. Quit your complaining and moaning."

"Our people consistently don't show up on time for work. Let's write a new policy for the employee handbook and start writing them up when they are late. That'll show em!"

"The best hires have college degrees and preferably an MBA."

"Marketing is the department responsible for creative ideas. We will give them 100% responsibility for our company's messaging strategy."

"Why would we have a Facebook Fan page?"

"Follow the leader. Don't make waves, don't ask questions, blend in and don't get noticed."

"It's a down economy. Let's just tighten our grip on things and stop innovating."

"Hierarchy is good, makes sense, and people need it."

"Mission statements matter."

What would you add to the list? Put YOUR favorite "Plan A" language here:

_____
_____
_____
_____

But this way of thinking is not limited to the way organization's think. Plan A thinking impacts individuals as well. When working one-on-one with professionals over the years--despite their industry, profession, business model they work in, gender, education level, age, or shoe size- these are some of the common things I hear:

"What do you mean I shouldn't use a PowerPoint for my five minute presentation? Why would I not use a PowerPoint? Everyone is going to use a PowerPoint."

"Yeah I have always wanted to go back to school and get a teaching certificate. Maybe one day..."

"Staying at home with my kids is just a dream. I gotta stay in this job that I hate and makes me miserable because we need the money."

"I hate my job but don't have options."

"I deserve a promotion and a raise. If they don't hurry up and realize it I am outta here."

"They would never consider me for that position. Who am I kidding?"

"I don't deserve it."

"So-and-So is far more qualified than me. I am sure they will go with him."

"I have this idea....." (that the person only talks about but never does anything about!)

"I really want to tell my boss _____" (but they never do!)

"I can't believe they fired me. I had no idea!"

I could fill another ten pages with these kinds of statements.

My point is this: Plan A thinking happens on an organizational level, a team/ departmental level, and an individual level. For too many people, it becomes a way of life. People, teams, and organizations live in a constant state of reaction being at the mercy of circumstances that they feel are out of their control. A client tells me "I don't know why we are wasting our time and energy on this presentation; the board has already made up their mind on who they are picking." This statement is simply code for "this is the way we have always done things. We will keep doing things this way and continue to scratch our heads and heavily sigh over getting our butts kicked by the competition again and again."

An extended example

One of the HOT TOPICS in training and development today is generations in the workplace. I love teaching this workshop, but I have to do a very good job of time management because when you get three (sometimes four) generations in the same room together it can become a finger pointing festival versus a learning opportunity. The laundry list of complaints missile launched from one generation into the lap of the other generations is really just a magnified example of Plan A thinking. Let me illustrate with the 40-hour work week.

For generations, the concept of the 40-hour work week has been embraced by corporate America. Arrive at 8:00 am and leave at 5:00 pm. My parents generation, the Traditionalists, advocated the time card system as a means of making sure the American worker logged the expected number of hours each day.

Generations at a Glance

Traditionalists: Born 1925 to 1942
Baby Boomers: Born 1943 to 1960
Gen X'ers: Born 1961 to 1980
Gen Y: Born 1981 to 2000
*Gen Y is more commonly referred to as Millennials

Along came the Baby Boomers and the concept of "work more than 40 hours a week to show how loyal you are to the organization" was born. Suddenly, the American worker (in corporate America primarily, but it shows up other places too) was working 50, 60, and sometimes 70 hours a week. For the most part, Gen X carried on this tradition, and as our culture changed and our excessive consumerism rose sharply we created a Plan A way of thinking that dictated: You need to earn as much money as possible to maintain your lifestyle, and that means working around the clock, coming in on the weekend, giving up your two-weeks vacation, and missing your kid's school play because you gotta get that report out of the office before business begins again tomorrow. (As a side note: Gen X was the generation that were the ones to collectively embrace and offer the idea of work-life balance. In working with my clients, I can say, anecdotally speaking of course, that there is a decided split in this generation between those who continue to advocate the work-life balance philosophy and those who have "gone to the dark side" if you will, and embraced the "work yourself to the point of mental and physical exhaustion" philosophy.

Then those trouble making Millennials came to town.

While we were were working ourselves to death, living on Rolaids and Red Bull--the next generation of American workers were taking notes. They arrived fresh-faced and packing a whole set of expectations that challenged "this is how we have always done things." A number of Gen Xers like myself got on board with their new-fangled ideas while other Gen Xers, Boomers, and Traditionalists were calling people like me and screaming "Come and sort these kids out!"

The introduction of a new generation to the workplace is one of the incubators for shifts in Plan A thinking. I love it. I love studying these shifts: researching, teaching, and connecting the dots between how these changes are challenging our Plan A thinking.

Every generation has it's own unique "voice" of who they are and what it means to belong to this particular group of people born during the same period. While I may be a Gen Xer, perhaps you belong to a different generation. What was the Plan A script for your generation? Did it limit you in any way in terms of your aspirations (My mom's generation for example were told girls could go to college to be a. teacher b. nurse or c. earn an M.R.S degree.)

1. What EVENTS (both national and international) shaped your generation and it's values?

2. What PEOPLE/FIGURES shaped your generation and it's values (think politics, entertainment, music, writers, etc.)?

3. What was Plan A for your generation?

4. In what ways, if any, were you IMPACTED or felt limited by this Plan A script?

5. How is your generation uniquely different from other generations?

Where are some other places where we can locate "Plan A" thinking being re-examined or re-considered given the changes in our cultural landscape? How about parenting. Ah yes, the age-old profession of being mommy/daddy to another human being.

When I became a mother the first time, thirteen years ago, I was surprised by how many women in my demographic were choosing to stay home with their children. After all, we were the most college-degreed generation of women in history! Many of us were raised by late generation Traditionalists and Baby Boomer moms who had fought to establish their place in corporate America with the hopes that their daughters would not face the same institutional (and sometimes legal) challenges they were up against in forging their career paths.

I watched my fill of 1970s and 1980s television shows with newly empowered women who were calling the shots in their own lives and on their own terms. I am the Oprah generation. Interestingly enough, however, I noticed when my oldest daughter Madeline was born that many women in my generation were opting out of the corporate hamster wheel to stay home with their little ones.

Linda Hirshman, retired women's studies professor at Brandeis University and author of *Get to work....and Get a Life Before it's too Late*, did an inspired study in 1996 at the height of the *Sex and the City* craze to test her theory that highly educated women were leaving the workplace to stay home with their children.

She writes:

"I -- a 1970s member of the National Organization for Women (NOW), a donor to EMILY's List, and a professor of women's studies -- did not set out to find this. I stumbled across the story when, while planning a book, I happened to watch Sex and the City's Charlotte agonize about getting her wedding announcement in the 'Sunday Styles' section of The New York Times. What better example, I thought, than the brilliantly educated and accomplished brides of the "Sunday Styles," circa 1996? At marriage, they included a vice president of client communication, a gastroenterologist, a lawyer, an editor, and a marketing executive.

In 2003 and 2004, I tracked them down and called them. I interviewed about 80 percent of the 41 women who announced their weddings over three Sundays in 1996. Around 40 years old, college graduates with careers: Who was more likely than they to be reaping feminism's promise of opportunity? Imagine my shock when I found almost all the brides from the first Sunday at home with their children. Statistical anomaly? Nope. Same result for the next Sunday. And the one after that.

Ninety percent of the brides I found had had babies. Of the 30 with babies, five were still working full time. Twenty-five, or 85 percent, were not working full-time. Of those not working full time, 10 were working part time but often a long way from their prior career paths. And half the married women with children were not working at all."

The 2000 census shows a trend worth noting: The numbers of women with infants who work full time is declining. The numbers play out as follows: 31 percent in 1976, the percentage had gone up almost every year to 1992, hit a high of 58.7 percent in 1998, and then began to drop -- to 55.2 percent in 2000, to 54.6 percent in 2002, to 53.7 percent in 2003. Statistics just released showed further decline to 52.9 percent in 2004.

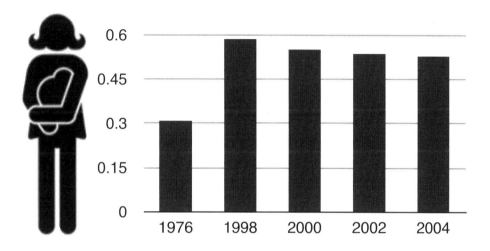

# of Women with Infants Working Full Time/2000 US. Census

| | 1976 | 1998 | 2000 | 2002 | 2004 |

Even the percentage of working mothers with children who were not infants declined between 2000 and 2003, from 62.8 percent to 59.8 percent. More women are CHOOSING to stay home with their children (There is NO judgement in this truth. It is only an observation of what is happening).

Now here is where I think this trend gets interesting. As the numbers of women have been declining in the world of full-time workers, a new phenomenon has steadily been growing at the same time: the trend of the stay-at-home Dad.

When in history has there been a movement of men challenging the notion of fatherhood in such a substantial and game-changing way as the idea that a Dad can stay home with his children and be the primary care giver? Never, that's when. But why is this happening? Good question.

I came across a wonderful blog that asked the question: "What is the hardest part of being a man today?" A few comments jumped out at me:

"Almost every aspect of our lives can be faked with technology, or presented in a veil of irony. It's gotten to the point where we are so suspicious or jaded or distracted that it's hard for any idea, relationship, piece of creative work, skill, or personality to really stand out or have any lasting value in today's world." --Carson Wright.

"I think it's gotten so bad that we don't even know who our genuine selves are. Kind of like the old saying, "If you repeat the lie enough times, it becomes the truth." We're so good at putting up a facade and handling things on a surface level that we forget the skill of introspection." --Jamie

"Perhaps you are blessed to be surrounded by a community of genuinely strong, confident, and polite gentlemen, but I see men struggle with society's neutered expectations of them every day. I am 25. I grew up with few good examples of real masculinity, and have watched most of my friends drift listlessly through life unable to commit to anything more than which video game to buy. The media caricature of modern men is representative of modern expectations of men. These are the traits society values today, and there has been little resistance from men."
--Gregory Garland

A new generation of men are writing a new set of rules in the arena of fatherhood and the concept of the SAHD (stay-at-home Dad) is becoming less of an oddity and more of an accepted aspect of the parenting world. If you pay any attention to advertising, you will see this shift. Men are now being portrayed in commercials, from diapers to domestic duties, as the lead character--something you would have not seen even twenty years ago.

The idea of a SAHD was unheard of when I was growing up in the 1970s and 1980s. So foreign a concept, I suspect that I would have tormented a kid who had a SAHD. Sad but true. But today the concept is gaining momentum. In his thought provoking book, *The Daddy Shift*, Jeremy Adam Smith explores the changing landscape of the American family by way of the SAHD.

Smith argues that as our world becomes more and more complicated and complex, so too do our notions of gender identify. Smith posits that the number of SAHDs in America must continue to rise to meet these demands. The SAHD is a movement of families writing a new set of rules (an emerging Plan Be) for what it means to be a parent--and more specifically what it means to be a father.

And the numbers are growing. In 2006 there were 159,000 SAHDs, but Dr. Aaron Rochlen, a counseling psychologist in The University of Texas at Austin's College of Education, points out that getting an accurate number is difficult because of how the census counts a SAHD. Regardless of the exact numbers, research from interested parties like Dr. Rochlen are finding positive correlations between SAHDs and the development of their children.

Likewise, Dr. Rocheln has found positive outcomes for the fathers themselves. One participant in a research study by Dr. Rocheln and his team shared, "There is not a day that it feels like I go to work. I still feel like I'm getting away with something. There's such sweetness to that...these are very pleasant days."

In sum, the increasing numbers of stay-at-home parents in general points toward a changing understanding of what it means to parent and how one thinks about work/life balance.

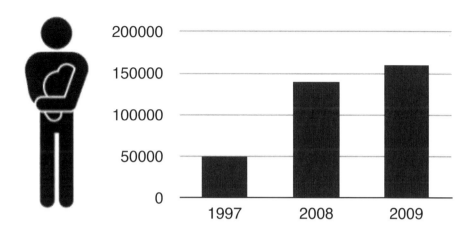

# of Stay at Home Dads/US Census Bureau Statistics

Whether it is the generational changes happening in today's organizations or the changing landscape of parenting in the United States, Plan A thinking is powerful and will often resist these changes. Plan A thinking, however, is not written on stone tablets. Change is possible. The two examples explored here--generations in the workplace and the changes in parenting philosophy over the last two decades-- are clear indications that "this is how we have always done things" can and does change. The challenge is the ability to recognize when it is time to "move on" and write a new rule for a new day. You will learn how to do that in the pages to come.

When my mom was a young professional working in a conservative, small-town bank, there was a strict dress code in place for the women working there. The stories she told me remind me a lot of the series *Mad Men* and the way the women dress on this show--girdles and all. In the 1980s, when colored pantyhose were popular, the bank where she worked came out with a rule that the women working there could not wear this new fashion trend of blue, green, red, pink, and other brightly colored pantyhose to work. When my mom told me that story, I was not struck by the stupidity of the rule, "No colored pantyhose," but the fact that they were expected to wear pantyhose at all! "You had to wear pantyhose every day?" I asked.

"Well of course!" she replied. Her generation is a generation that wore panty hose. Mine is not. I cannot even tell you the last time I had on a pair of panty hose. I will now add to my gratitude list: Lord thank you for letting me live in a world where I don't have to wear pantyhose to work.

Pantyhose is not going to make or break a person, I know that. But I do believe that the power of Plan A thinking can do damage. A lot of damage.

Plan A Will Kill Us All

It is worth noting that Plan A is not inherently BAD. My intention is not to suggest to you that you "torch the village" and start from scratch. (But you might want to throw all your pantyhose in the trash! Especially if you are a man wearing them to work.)

My intentions are more complex. What I am asking of you is to recognize Plan A thinking and then set out to decide if these ideas that have become accepted as fact in your life are helping you or limiting you. When the answer is, "This is limiting me," then it is time to do the hard work of evolving.

I love the mantra "Evolve or Die."

If we embrace the idea of evolving, it is fundamentally important to also understand the complexity between our Plan A modes of thinking, professionally and personally. The two

Plan A:

Is this limiting me?
Is this limiting my team?
Is this limiting my organization?
Is this limiting my family?

are so intertwined today that it is often hard to separate them. Fifty years ago the divide between the personal and the professional was somewhat easy to maintain. You went to work, did your job, came home at night and lather, rinse, and repeat five days a week. The concept of "taking your work home" or working 12-to-14 hour days was not common practice, and remember, this was pre-technology when it was easy to leave work at work.

Spend five minutes in the grocery store check-out lane and take a moment to read the headlines of today's popular magazines. They are a fascinating illustration of how overwhelmed we are as a culture. Headlines are riddled with articles on stress, managing your weight, worries over the future, finding time for your family, reconnecting to your spouse or partner, and looking good while you do it all. It's over-freakin'-whelming.

Yes, it may seem like a bit of hyperbole, but I do think that the damage that has been done to us in trying to live up to the expectations and rules of Plan A, which we had no say in creating, has many people feeling deflated. Plan A gets handed down from one generation to the next. Small changes happen, but substantial changes are slow to materialize. I don't think there are any new challenges that come our way compared to people living in decades passed, they are just new flavors of the same pressures, predicaments, and problems. Most of us reach a point where we acknowledge that there is a yearning inside of us to do something new. Something different. If you have felt like, "This is not what I signed up for," and it scares the %&*# out of you, then you understand the power of Plan A.

The way this harsh dose of medicine sometimes gets resolved is with the classic mid-life crisis. "Feed me!" my ego tells me. "Make me feel good right now!" it demands of us. And so instead of squarely facing the tough, painful questions that are holding us back from living our best selves, we instead opt out and allow material items, drugs, alcohol, gambling, infidelity, and other vices to fill the void. What's Your Plan Be? is my attempt to help you answer those questions for yourself (your family, your team, your organization) and apply the concepts within this little ol' book to your life.

We can choose the mid-life crisis (or quarter-life crisis that John Mayer sings about so eloquently. Yes, he is a giant bone-head, but the man is a poet!), or we can choose to take control of our destiny. Everyone at some point has wondered: Is this all there is?

And while the challenges each of us face are in many ways the same as they were for our parents, grandparents, and great-grand parents, I think our modern day culture has some notable distinctions. We are the most educated generations of people in the history of education (essentially the dawn of time), and the most "plugged-in" generation of adults as well. Many of us are dying slow deaths from all the material items we have; the overload of information in our face all day, every day; and the personal and professional demands placed on us.

Here are a few sobering facts about our "modern world"

1. According to the International Labor Organization "Americans work 137 more hours per year than Japanese workers, 260 more hours per year than British workers, and 499 more hours per year than French workers."

2. Most American workers report that they regularly check email during family outings and dinners, when they get up in the morning and when they go to bed at night. According to the Huffington Post, these little "extras" **add up to an extra seven hours of work a week.**

3. Doctors are now reporting patients experiencing negative health effects from their overuse of technology. Headaches, anxiety, and depression are now being linked to technology dependence. Yikes!

4. We are in debt up to our eyeballs. Consider student loan debt for a moment. The majority of borrowers still paying back their loans are in their thirties or older and carry a total outstanding debt of $902 billion (American Student Assistance).

5. We are overweight. The Centers for Disease control note that of the Americans over the age of twenty, 35.9% are considered obese and 33.3% are considered overweight.

6. We are over-medicated. *Forbes* magazine asked the question "are Americans overmedicated?" and here is what they found: Nearly half of women ages 20-44 are being treated for chronic conditions, in addition to one-third of men their age.

Top treatments used by the general public include medications for high cholesterol and high blood pressure, with use of cholesterol drugs by 20- to 44-year-old men increasing by more than 80% over the past seven years. And nearly 30% of children ages 19 and under take a chronic medication.

Are you still unclear on how our Plan A world is killing us? In my estimation, our Plan A reality has resulted in the most over scheduled + over committed + over stimulated generations in our history. ALL of history!

Have you noticed that one of the major headline topics in 2010 was about SLEEP? Sleep. Are you kidding me? But a number of medical research studies over the last decade have revealed that the lack of sleep for the average American is alarming. A recent article in *Business Week* draws a picture of who we are right now:

> More than 31% of college-educated male workers are regularly logging 50 or more hours a week at work, up from 22% in 1980. Forty percent of American adults get less than seven hours of sleep on weekdays, reports the National Sleep Foundation, up from 31% in 2001. About 60% of us are sometimes or often rushed at mealtime, and one-third wolf down lunch at our desks.

So add lack of sleep to the list.

We are working too much, eating too much, taking too many medications, stressed by our growing dependence on technology, and we are tired. Really tired.

I am guessing that as you read through this list you were considering yourself in the context of these issues. Take me for example. I struggle with the sleep category. I am a small business owner, mother of two girls who seem to constantly need to be driven somewhere, and married to a husband that travels. There are consequences that come with my oh-so-modern lifestyle.

I am always challenged by my use (overuse) of technology. I was at my daughter's dance convention this weekend when her dance teacher came up to me in the lobby and said, "I never see you without your phone in your hand." It was embarrassing. It was true. I gotta work on that one. Note to self: put your phone down!

Two years ago, I set an alarm on my phone to go off every weekday at 5:00pm that says "Shut your computer and put your phone down. Engage with your family." Sad? Yes. But our connectivity means we can work anytime, anywhere, and for some of us it has created a new way to disengage from reality. Reality being those truly meaningful relationships with family and friends. You know--those people that love you in spite of yourself?

My own experiences are where Plan Be was birthed. Plan Be is for you, but it is for me too. Like so many people, the constant struggle to find that elusive thing called balance in my personal and professional life compels me to institute a set of practices that keep me focused and moving toward my goals. It is too easy to get side tracked, distracted, and over-committed, and the consequence is we are robots living on auto pilot. I don't want to be a robot. I don't want to live on auto pilot. Do you? I know you don't.

The first step is for us is to take a more reflective point of view of our own lives (or our organizations), and identify the places where Plan A thinking is hurting us instead of helping us. We can, but we shouldn't, champion ideas that are fabrications and lies, pretending that they are working for us. A great example where I see this play out again and again is in our celebration of being "stressed out." Far too many people wear their stress like it is a badge of honor. We revel in telling people how busy our lives are and our superpower, hero like ability to "manage" our stress. In some messed up way we believe stress is a sign of our importance in the world.

This concept is not only true for professionals but for some stay-at-home moms I know too. I love Jennifer Weiss' explanation in an opinion piece in the *Daily Pennsylvanian*. She writes, "We live in a culture of stress. In this culture, if you're not stressed, you're boring. You're not sufficiently important, interesting, popular or smart to fill your schedule with twice as many activities as can be completed in 24 hours. Stress is a measure of personal success, and discussing your stress is a convenient, veiled way to talk about how important you are."

Let me give an example to illustrate.

A few years ago, Dallas/Ft. Worth was hit hard by a winter storm that lasted for a long five days. A friend's husband insisted on driving into work despite the conditions. Dallas/Ft. Worth had virtually shut down. The streets, interstates, and highways were covered in a thick coating of ice, and the local news warned "travel at your own peril." Her husband, however, could not conceive of staying at home and chose to drive a good ways from home to office.

But there was no work to really be done. All his clients stayed at home!

Meetings were canceled, and parents were enjoying the beautiful snow with their kids. I am diagnosing from afar, but in my own estimation, he suffered from a bad case of Plan A. Plan A says those who are truly committed go into work. Plan A says work first, family second. When my friend shared this story with me, she pointed out that almost all the men at his office came into work too, and all the women stayed home. Plan A would say "typical women, their priorities are obviously in the wrong place." Plan Be would offer a different explanation.

You understand the impact that Plan A thinking has on us as individuals, so now let's turn our attention to how Plan A hurts organizations as well. I have already touched on a few ideas where Plan A thinking shows up in organizations. "Talent retention" is a popular term in the Human Resources (HR) world these days as more and more pressure is placed on organizations to do more with less. I work with a lot of talented people, and here is what they are telling me: "I am tired," "I am stressed out," "I work sun up to sun down and I don't know how much longer I can take it," "I hate my job," "My boss just doesn't seem to understand all the pressure I am under," and, "I work until midnight and still can't get everything done."

If they don't come out and tell me these things, I see it in their faces, their body language, and the knowing glances they exchange with one another when they are in a training room with me for a workshop. It appears to me, from an outsider's perspective, that the idea of talent retention is just that--an idea. The practice of talent retention has a ways to go.

Plan A thinking can be impacted by a down economy in ways that will be felt by the organization for generations to come. When the economy is down, Plan A thinking kicks into high gear and you hear things like, "They should just be glad they have a job," "We can't afford to hire on another person, just let Bob do Sally's job too," "It's not like they are going to go out and find another job in this economy right?", and other incredibly ineffective ways of thinking. And by "incredibly ineffective" I mean downright stupid.

And yes, just to clarify--I have been told, "They should just be happy they have a job," by a client. I waited till I got to my car to yell and scream, cuss, and roll my eyes.

PLAN A SAYS:	CONSEQUENCES OF PLAN A
9-to-5 still makes sense.	*Lose out on talent that are not able to work a traditional 9-to-5 job. *Resentment from employees who cannot maintain work life balance because of a rigid work environment
People at the top of the food chain have figured it all out and don't need training and development sense.	*Leadership becomes stale because they are not working on their skills set and evolving with the changing marketplace. *Employees resent leadership because they are not required to attend training.
Annual performance reviews are effective.	*Employees are caught off guard by criticism of things that happened 6, 9, or event 12-months ago. *Managers struggle to give constructive feedback because they can't remember what happened over the last 12 months; therefore, no true and meaningful development happens for the employee! *Review feels like a trip to the principal's office versus an ongoing dialogue on finding opportunities for growth.

Reconsider three items from my earlier laundry list of Plan A thinking at the organizational level, but now think of it in terms of "Truth and Consequences." The bottom line consequences of Plan A thinking for organizations looks like this:

1. Your employees are uninspired and bored. When people are uninspired + bored they stop innovating, asking questions, and dreaming.
2. An organization that is empty of innovators and dreamers will begin to lose market share as their competition swoops in and takes clients away.
3. When you lose clients, you lose money.
4. When you lose enough money, you go out of business.

The truth and consequences of Plan A is a risky game to play, and there is no new washer and dryer set that goes to the winner of this game. There are only losers when using Plan A thinking to operate in a marketplace that has moved forward.

In sum, Plan A thinking impacts us as individuals and organizations.

INDIVIDUAL	ORGANIZATIONAL
Health Issues: stress, high blood pressure, overweight, loss of sleep.	Failure to hire and retain talent. Talented people gravitate to organizations that are dynamic and evolving.
Unsatisfactory relationships. When you don't know who you are, it is hard to connect to other people.	Innovation screeches to a halt. True innovators ask questions and are willing to take risks.
Addictions: Like it or not, the ego is going to find satisfaction one way or the other. When we don't do the hard to work to find what "gets us high" we will turn to other things to fill the void.	One step behind the competition all the time. Someone else will beat you to market every time and you will scramble to catch up.
Stagnate professionally. People who are not working toward something don't go anywhere.	Tackling the same issues over and over and over again while hoping for different results.
Make decisions from a place of fear. Finding Your Plan Be and living it takes courage. When you lack courage, you find fear is how you make choices.	Failed leadership. Leaders who lead from a place of fear impact the organization from top to bottom.
Blame everyone. People who let forces dictate their choices live in a state of blame and believe that everything that happens is out of their control.	Lost revenue. Organizations who live in reaction mode "Oh Plan A didn't work what is our Plan B?" lose money.

The take away is simple. Take the time to define YOUR Plan Be and then set yourself up with success measures to reach your plan. If you don't define your Plan Be for yourself, someone else will--society, culture, family, spouse, children, your boss, or your job. If you feel this sense of being unsettled in your life, stop for a moment and consider to what degree it could be because you have allowed someone else to define your plan. It's not too late to take the reigns and define it for yourself.

These realties are where Plan Be was born. More and more, I see women and men of all ages around me who seem unsettled. I have friends going through divorces, parents with kids who are growing up and becoming independent, and many of these friends are ready for the next chapter.

I work with organizations who are feeling the same emotions as the individuals who work for them. Things are changing and they worry they are getting left behind. But they aren't sure what the next chapter is, or should be, or could be, or will be. And many lack the courage to move forward, confront reality, talk out loud about the possibilities, and jump.

And fly.

This book may be a starting place for you to say out loud, "This is who I am! This is what I want! This is who I will be! Just watch me!"

Yes, I am getting a little touchy feely here, and that's OK. I am not asking you to go buy a crystal and meditate three hours a day (See p.45 for that. Just Kidding). I am asking something far more fundamental to who you are. You have a purpose. You have a responsibility to find that purpose. You have a duty to share it with the world and make the world a better place.

What if Picasso had never painted?

What if Martin Luther King had never told us his dream?

What if Maya Angelou never wrote, "I know why the caged bird sings"?

What if Marie Curie had never stepped into the research laboratory?

What if Barbara Streisand had never opened her mouth to sing (in spite of her crippling stage fright)?

What if Oprah Winfrey had said, "I am not good enough"?

So many what ifs. You probably have your own set of what ifs. What a sad day it will be when we get to the end of our journey and we are left with nothing but a big pile of what ifs.

I believe with a fierce and fiery passion that no one should sell themselves short or define their reality based on limitations set by someone else, and sit in the passenger seat while someone else drives the bus. And that is, in a nutshell, what I think Plan A is all about--letting something else define and limit our realities.

Your Plan Be is yours to find. Name it, Claim it, and Live it.

From the time we are able to form sentences we are asked, "What do you want to be when you grow up?" If you remember yourself as a little kid, I am sure your answers were a garden variety of things you were interested in at the time. How many kids say they want to be a veterinarian because they love their puppy? When we graduate from high school we are still asked this question, and I remember feeling overwhelmed by the expectations of all these adults waiting to hear about my big plans for the future. But I didn't really know what I wanted to be yet!

Name It.
Claim It.
Live It.

In college I watched my friends jump from one major to another, not quite sure what they were going to do post-college. Most of us just hoped we would get a good job that would pay us enough to rent a cool apartment and drive a great car. I was recently asked what I studied in college, and when I replied, "Both of my degrees are in communication studies," she replied, "Oh wow! You are someone who actually has a job doing what you studied!" Rare indeed!

This question of "Who do you want to be?" does not get asked much beyond twenty-two years old. We just assume that everyone knows who they want to be by that point. But the reality is just the opposite. I work with, and know a number of adults in their thirties, forties, and yes even in their fifties and sixties who don't know who they want to be. When I work with them professionally as their coach, my job is to help them answer what seems like such a simple question, but in the end proves to be far more complex than imagined.

"What's Your Plan Be?" is a dare to you. A dare to question boldly.

In his forthcoming book, *A More Beautiful Question*, Warren Berger explores the possibilities of growth by learning to ask more questions. On his accompanying website, he writes:

> Interestingly, we all start out as super-questioners—no one asks more questions than your average 5-year-old. But the habit of asking questions is trained out of us by the educational system. And then, as we make our way into the business world, we find that too often the emphasis is on short-term answers rather than exploring more far-reaching, potentially game-changing ideas. Research shows that many people in business are

actually afraid to question the way things are done because they fear it will make them seem incompetent. (http://amorebeautifulquestion.com)

Berger is on to something. To ask questions is to acknowledge that one does not have all the answers. That takes courage. It also takes permission. You must be ready to give yourself permission to go down that road that feels a little risky.

I had the great pleasure of working with a woman recently as her coach. Let's call her Barbara. Barbara brought me in initially to work with her on her storytelling abilities to more fully represent the interests and mission of her department within her organization. Our sessions were three hours at a time, which sounds like a long time to just sit around and talk, but I can tell you the time flew by.

In our first session, we covered a lot of ground, and it became clear within the first few minutes that she was up against a lot of "stuff": politics, personalities, agendas, and a changing landscape in her field. In our second session, two months later, much of what we had talked about came to a head, and she had a lot to catch me up on. Her focus had moved away from our initial reason for meeting toward a more personal plan for how she would respond given these changes that she had no control over. When I pointed out what she did have control over was her decisions, she smiled a wicked smile. "I knew you would say that," and she laughed.

I think she knew before we spoke what she was supposed to do but, having someone outside of her organization, who was not invested in these dynamics, helped her talk through different scenarios and choices that were available. As is often the case, the choice she felt she was meant to make was also the one that was the scariest and would mean a lot of changes for her in her life both personally and professionally. She laughed several times as she settled in to her decision. It was time for a new chapter and the universe had sent her multiple "gifts" with her name clearly stamped on them. The ball was in her court.

Ultimately, Barbara found her courage and is now transitioning into a new adventure. She embraced the idea that she could be something new.

These are the kinds of stories that inspire me to encourage people to ask the right questions.

In the following pages I will share with you the process to find Your Plan Be. I have had the good fortune to work with many people in a professional capacity as a consultant over the past eight years. Likewise, as a college professor and self described lifetime student, I have studied human communication both as an avid fan of people and how they behave, and with a critical eye that comes from my time in academia. I am always learning more, reading, considering, and analyzing. And I ask A LOT of questions. All of these things have shaped the way I designed the process to find your Plan Be.

One key element of the process is to learn through other people's experiences and stories. Many of the stories I will share are stories of success. I know a lot of stories of failure too (including my own), and will share a few, changing names, dates, and details to protect the interests of those who experienced the failure. Through both the sharing of the good and the bad, I hope to illuminate what I believe are some key qualities to finding your Plan Be. Likewise, I have brought in relevant blog posts Bravo cc that compliment each topic and provide further insight to finding your Plan Be.

Let me be crystal clear--this is not a cookie cutter formula for success. I don't believe in formulas when it comes to human behavior. In math 2 + 2 always = 4. But in the world of humans that doesn't mean if I copy the same strategy as another person, I will get the same results they do. We are too dynamic and trying to bottle success is a difficult and often defeating experience. Instead, this book is simply a glimpse into a series of activities I use with my clients to help them answer the question: Who do you want to Be? Instead of a formula, look at it as a process.

This book is meant to help you find Your Plan Be for yourself personally, professionally, and can be applied to your team, department, or organization. To do that, I have designed the content of the book carefully with the goal of giving you interesting ways to "connect" to the material. You will see:

ACTIVITIES
to give you the chance to stop, reflect, and apply to concepts to your life

BLOG POSTS
that are related to the content in the chapter

RESOURCE LIST
I LOVE learning new things and these resource lists will give you great follow up information beyond the book

So let's get started! I have had my coffee today, I walked the dog, my kids are at school learning to be productive members of society (fingers crossed), and I have Michael Jackson playing on Pandora. Pretty perfect conditions for writing.

PLAN BE ACTIVITY TIME.

Stepping into the shallow end of the pool just to get started.

Take a few quiet minutes to reflect on the following questions and consider where you are at right now in your life. Be honest because playing games with yourself won't get you anywhere!

Is there a longing or desire in you that you have been afraid to speak out loud? What is it?

Do you have a history of setting goals for yourself?

Do you tend to complete or abandon these goals?

Do you use a process for goal setting that has proven useful to you in the past?

Right here and right now, what is keeping you from going after your hidden desire, dream, hope, unfulfilled wish?

What are THREE things you could do right now to move you toward fulfilling this desire, dream, hope, or unfulfilled wish?

BLOG EXTRA!
The Myth of the Wonder Woman Super Mommy!

My FAVORITE superhero is by far Wonder Woman! Linda Carter played Wonder Woman on the campy TV series in the late 1970s and I thought she was amazingly beautiful, strong, powerful, and heroic--I wanted to be her! I never got superhero powers (or a nose wiggle that would make things happen like Samantha on Bewitched), but that did not keep me from trying to achieve Wonder Woman status. Today, with a little wisdom and experience, I have to resist trying to be Wonder Woman Super Mommy!

When I look around, I see women like me trying to be Wonder Woman Super Mommy everywhere. And that has inspired today's post.

Why? Well here is what I think:

The number of women to men in the college classroom has now taken a turn. There are more women going to college, more graduating from college, and more going to graduate school. Historically male dominated degree programs like engineering, architecture, medicine, accounting, and law are seeing a noticeable shift in their numbers too. When our own daughters head to college there will be more degreed women in our country than men, and this is going to change the landscape of business life and home life in ways that we (the fully emancipated generation!) cannot imagine.

And yet, despite how well educated women are today and despite how emancipated we are, the urge to mother our young is not lost on all these degreed women. When I had my first daughter, I was 26 years old with a bachelor's and master's degree. After all that hard work on my education, I looked at my husband and told him,"I will not leave this little person at daycare or with another person. Period."

Staying home with my kids was top priority. Blessed with my degrees, I was able to teach two days a week for about four hours each day, which allowed me to spend the bulk of my time with my girls. Even today with a ten- and eight-year-old, I work from home (ok Starbucks), and my goal is "be there when the school bell rings" at the end of the day. I want my kids to have mom at home.

Now, all of this is going somewhere. I promise. Being this highly accessible mom to my kids makes me very prone to feelings that I am supposed to somehow be Wonder Woman Mommy all the time. I think about things I feel certain my mom never gave a thought to when I was young: lining up play dates, having the right snacks at home after school, taking my kids to all the culturally relevant events in our city, worrying over report cards and homework, and planning fun and stimulating things for summer! Wonder Woman Mommy to the rescue!

What has happened is that in many ways I (and my peers) have turned the raising of our children into our profession. We are professional child raisers.

Now I have a theory on why this is the case: Most of the women I live around are middle class and have degrees or at least went to college. I think that perhaps these two things combine to create the Wonder Woman Mommy challenge that so many of us succumb to.

Working or Working at home or Working from home-- every mother I encounter these days holds herself to a standard that is ultimately debilitating. I am not suggesting that ALL mothers suffer from this Wonder Woman Super Mommy myth OK? Some don't. I don't think my mom did. I don't think she laid in bed at night and wondered if she was screwing up her kids. I think she did the best she could. And her best was good enough. It really was. I never felt like a project to her. She did not manage my social life or invest in my education to the degree that I felt smothered.

With all this being said, here is my take on the Wonder Woman Super Mommy myth:

1. We are not doing our kids any favors managing every aspect of their lives. We are already seeing the impact of helicopter parents on kids coming out of college. These kids can't function! They are moving back home with mommy and daddy because no one taught them to be independent.

2. The Wonder Woman Super Mommy is downright afraid of letting her young fail. But there is great character development in failure. We must, must, must let our kids fail sometimes. And look I am not talking drugs, sex, etc. I am talking our kid leaves their library book at home and cries because she won't get to check out a book so we go back home, search for the stupid book, and drive it back up to school (look I have done this! I am telling myself this as much as anyone else). We need to let our kids see how if feels to sit there in the library and not check out a book. I think if we let them learn the consequences of these little failures then maybe the SUPER BIG LIFE ALTERING FAILURES won't happen when they become teenagers and young adults. They learned early what it means to have consequences to their choices.

3. The Wonder Woman Super Mommy believes she must keep her young stimulated at all times. Now, reflect on your formative years. How much of it was spent exploring outside, "free play" with friends, creating your own world in your bedroom or at the park? Our kids are losing out on this necessary and good part of life because Wonder Woman Super Mommy spends so much time creating her kid's over scheduled lives.

4. The Wonder Woman Super Mommy is afraid of everything and everyone. At some point we have to start giving our kids some space to roam and explore and seek adventure. Statistically speaking the chances of your kid being abducted are

low. And if we prepare our kids and make them smart then we can give them some freedom to be out there in the world.

5. The Wonder Woman Super Mommy thinks anything less than perfect is failure. So your kid didn't make straight As this six weeks. Who cares? And again I ask Who cares? The research and evidence is clear: Your child's success in their adult life will not be ultimately determined their GPA or their IQ. Their emotional and social intelligence will play a far larger role in their success. No lie--it's worth a Google.

These are just a few of the "powers" of the Wonder Woman Super Mommy that leave us actually feeling drained, overwhelmed, and well, powerless. This is a touchy subject. Talking about moms and pointing the finger (at myself really more than anyone else) is a risky business. But it is a topic worth talking about. When we try to be Wonder Woman Mommy, we fall into the trap of letting the sum of our worth rest in our mommy-hood, and we often make the terrible mistake of holding other women to our Wonder Woman Super Mommy standards.

So today, take off the cape for a minute and rest and relax. It might just make you feel powerful.

BLOG EXTRA!
An Open Letter to My Girls

Dear Maddie and Trinity,

This is a love letter.

The word on the street is my generation of parents are simply ruining our kids. The popular terminology is "helicopter parent," and there are now countless articles, books, and experts out there pontificating on how we have gotten it wrong. You know the parent--they can't let their little one out of their sight for a moment, they do everything they can to keep their kid from experiencing any kind of pain or failure, they micro-manage their kid's friendships, activities, food intake, grades, etc. Our generation of parents fully child-proofed our homes, made our own baby food, sat in the classroom with our kids the first week of school to make sure they were adjusting, and going so far as to text their kid's teacher every day for a status report.

If helicopter parenting is defined as "over-parenting" then you might describe my parenting style as "under-parenting" (which sounds just awful!). But I want you to understand WHY I do the things I do.

When I say things like "I don't want to be your friend. That's not my job. My job is to be your parent," I hope you know that one day I want to be your friend. But for now we need to maintain like an 80/20 split. I am 80% parent and 20% friend. As you age and mature that will change.

When I make you do chores, I hope you understand it is because I see your future. I am always thinking about your future, and in your future self I want to know you will be OK living on your own, keeping your "space," and you have a sense of pride in your surroundings.

I hope you understand that when you ask me to go up to the school and give that mean teacher the what for that you understand I don't because I need you to learn to fight your battles. The truth is that you are always going to have a teacher (boss, co-worker, client) that you just don't like, and you've gotta learn to get along with them. It's just the way life works.

Do you get that I don't check your grades on line because quite simply I don't see that as my job or responsibility? You are smart, and you do well in school. School is your job. Your grades are your pay check. If you come home with a bad grade, that is on you and ultimately you will pay the price, not me. Will I help you any time you need help? You better believe it! But I won't do the work for you, and I won't hover over you every night to make sure you are doing what you are supposed to. Because I don't intend to come to your job every day and see if you are doing what you should be doing right? So this is where you will establish the ability to be self-directed and take care of business.

And let me tell you this:

You two are simply the greatest kids I have ever known. Maddie your quick wit and sense of yourself floors me. You are so much more sophisticated than I was at 13. I love that you have spent so much time teaching yourself about hair and makeup, and sister I can just see you in ten years doing this for Hollywood Celebrities. I love that you think about your future and you plan for it. You have changed so very much over the last year, and you are truly coming into yourself. As your mom it has been a real joy to watch. Do you know that I look up to you? I really do. I am inspired by you and your passions.

Trinity, at my fundraiser this year when you embraced the woman who was there by herself and got her in the photo booth with you--well it just brings me to tears. That woman came all alone and earlier that day had told me that she really needed to be there. I could tell she was in emotional pain. When she came and told me that you had basically told her "we are going to be friends" it is one of the proudest moments I have had being your mom. Your tender heart makes me more tender hearted. Thank you for that.

I am so proud that people compliment us on what great manners you girls have. We have been training you since you could walk and talk to be able to interact with adults, and now we are seeing our efforts pay off.

Now do you see that I am a "mean" parent because I love you. My "under-parenting" is the direct result of being in the college classroom teaching kids who had been over-parented and seeing the effects it had on these kids. I have made a very deliberate attempt to go in a different direction in my own parenting. I also know that every person on this planet is going to experience pain and heartache and failure and frustration and that is where our character gets built. I would not be doing you any favors if I protected you from every little thing that the world is going to bring your way.

I love you. To the moon and back. You are the best thing that has ever happened to me, and being your mom is the best job I have ever had. And I am sorry I yelled all the way from the drive way at home to dropping you at school. And I appreciate you telling me you love me when you got out even if you weren't feeling it.

Your mom.

P.S. Please do the dishes and walk the dog when you get home from school :)

BLOG EXTRA!
Talkin' Bout My Generation

with Guest Blogger Jake Thompson, twenty-something professional

One of the most common retorts I hear from my clients is "these young kids have no work ethic" or some other version like this. It is funny because that has not been my experience. "Those young kids" are certainly a different generation, and the ways in which they work and play are different from generations past. Their philosophy of work is different too. It has been my experience that many of "these young kids" are not willing to sell their souls to their jobs. What is happening? Essentially the "older generation" of Baby Boomers and Gen Xers are feeling challenged because a generation of Millennials are rejecting Plan A.

Let's imagine for a moment why that might be? Hmmmmm.....

1. Many of the men and women in the Millennial generation grew up with two working parents. That means they went to day care while mom and dad worked 50, 60, 70+ hours a week. I think many of today's twenty-somethings don't want that for themselves because of the toll it took on their home life growing up.

2. At the same time this generation grew up seeing organizations become less and less loyal to their employees. Gone are the days of working your 40 years for the same organization and getting a gold watch when you retire. Today's worker will change jobs 5+ times in their career.

3. With the advances in technology, today's twenty something generation looks at getting work accomplished differently. You no longer have to be "in the office" to get work done. Unfortunately many employers still see "face time" as the measuring stick for effort.

4. Finally, I think today's twenty something worker does not live to work, they live to play. Work is a means to an end for many of them, and they are not going to live an unbalanced existence where they have no life outside of work.

I thought I would ask a twenty something professional to give me his thoughts on this. Below are some thoughts from Jake Thompson.

"The man who goes farthest is generally the one who is willing to do and dare. The sure-thing boat never gets far from the shore." – Dale Carnegie

The one thing I am consistently asked by colleagues and strangers is why, as a 26-year-old young professional, would I want to tackle the uphill challenge of being a freelance consultant in today's business world.

The answer can be a long, drawn out explanation that might include things about how my father built his company from the ground up and I feel it is a way I can honor my family's work history. Or I could share that I think my ADHD prevents me from sitting still in a cubicle all day. Or I could give you any number of creative excuses, but it ultimately came down to this – I wanted to use my God-given abilities in service and accomplish something that truly matters in a way that I felt best suited my abilities.

Heres the cliff notes on my journey. I graduated Texas Christian University in 2006 with my bachelor's degree in Advertising/Public Relations and from the University of Dallas with my MBA in Sports and Entertainment Business in 2008. Throughout college I began interning with a variety of sports organizations; including sports agencies, sports marketing groups, and professional teams. I volunteered at events and took an active role in the industry to learn everything I could. I always thought I wanted to be the next Jerry Maguire and was hell-bent on achieving that goal.

I began to feel the need to start my own sports marketing group after spending 2008 at a newer sports agency where I didn't see eye-to-eye with how things were handled and felt that the industry was corrupting me as an individual. I was not becoming the man I wanted to be and felt that in order to continue loving the game I had a passion for and to grow in my own personal life, I needed a split from the agent side of sports. The split from the agency led me to create AthElite Marketing.

I began with small graphic design and event planning projects through my personal network. As Bob Beaudine put it best in his book, *The Power of Who*, it was my "WHO" people who helped me get going. After struggling for a few months, one of my former graduate school professors referred me to an entertainment development project in Irving ,and I eventually signed on as a consultant with the project.

I have spent the last two years working with the city of Irving on their entertainment complex while continuing to build a base of sports-related clients with AthElite. I recently launched another website devoted to non-sports marketing and branding called Stacked.

I am very aware of the looks I get when walking into certain meetings because of my youth and am very conscious of the stigma of my generation. We are "lazy, apathetic about our jobs, impatient, and constantly searching for the next 'great' gig." My generation is perceived to be inexperienced, unwilling to roll up our sleeves and stay late, and on and on and on the list goes.

I will give some of the critics credit – there are members of my generation who fit every stereotype I just listed. But, there are also members of their generation and the generation before them who also fit these stereotypes. We can not all be lumped into the same barrel, just as those in the generation before us, and before them should be stereotyped by my generation. It is all a matter of perspective.

I think the biggest misperception between generations in the workplace is the way my generation was raised. We have had technology at our fingertips from the time we were young – video games, cell phones, laptops, and now social media. As a whole, society is becoming more and more dependent on the big three as their sole means of information – television, computer, and cell (or smart) phones. We want everything one minute ago, and we have become a culture of instant gratification.

My generation is accustomed to all of this information, and therefore was raised to work in a different manner than past generations. We do not know any other way.

We do not have to be sitting at a desk from 8-5 to be productive because everything we need is at our fingertips, making us mobile. Physical boundaries do not limit us. All the hustle and bustle, moving from here to there doesn't mean we are anxious or impatient, it just means we have the freedom to travel – a freedom we try to take advantage of.

Thanks to always-changing technologies, we can still be plugged into our work from anywhere. In fact, I get more work done at the local Starbucks with my headphones on at a corner table than I ever do at my office. There are too many people to socialize with and too many wasted minutes in meetings that do not require my presence.

This new generation is not one of laziness, but of freedom. We work just as hard, we just work differently. Unknown to most, our biggest challenge is not finding motivation to work, but making the opportunity to "unplug" and breathe, away from work.

It is almost impossible to leave your work at the office unless you make a conscious decision to. Every entrepreneur struggles with this. My father was always on the clock with his convenience stores because they were his stores and his responsibilities. My generation struggles with that as well, but in a different way because Blackberries, iPhones, and laptops instantaneously link us to the office, no matter where we are. Even vacations can easily turn into working trips with a simple email. I find myself going crazy if I don't consciously turn off my computer a night or two a week because I will get home from my office and immediately start doing more work on the couch.

There will always be individuals who prefer to sit at their desk, clock in and clock out of work, then go home. Corporate America needs that to excel. Like many others of my generation, all of this freedom has afforded me the ability to think creatively, outside of the box, and not be limited by four walls, much less the status quo. My parents always encouraged me to try harder, push myself farther, and be creative. I am not content in accepting second – in sports, in business, in life. I will fail, it is inevitable. But I know that nothing great has ever been achieved without a struggle, and my success and legacy will not be determined by my failures, but in overcoming those failures on my way to success.

If you are facing in the right direction, all you need to do is keep on walking.

Buddhist saying

FIND YOUR PLAN BE

I am a true believer in the power of PROCESS. Process becomes all the more necessary and good when you live in a time that the availability of information is truly overwhelming, competition in the marketplace is mind-numbing, our personal lives are complicated and complex, and there are more and more "experty experts" out there selling programs, books, T-shirts, and bumper stickers to help you realize your perfect life. How many times have you said to someone, "Well just Google it"? I say it all the time. I am tapped into to a dizzying array of resources on Facebook, Linked In, Twitter, and Slideshare. I can't begin to count how many people's daily, weekly, and monthly emails I have signed up for.

Recently I have been unsubscribing to a lot of these sources of information because I now have a handful of trusted resources I turn to time and time again for inspiration, education, information, and motivation. The rest turned out to be simply noise. I will share my resources that I use almost religiously throughout the book.

Now back to my philosophy on PROCESS.

I am a true believer in process. I think I mentioned that.

I have always been fascinated by the concept of the 12-step program used by Alcoholics Anonymous (AA), and a few years ago I spent some time thinking about the 12 steps and why they have been adopted by so many other organizations helping people fight addiction. I am convinced that the 12-step program works for millions of people because it provides a framework for people to move through as they learn to live with and manage their addiction.

In that spirit, here is why I KNOW that process is a necessary part of the success equation.

1. Process Lets You Flourish

People flourish when process is introduced into the equation. I remember when I was in pre-school and every morning the teacher would hold up a chart and sing a song about what we should do every day. "Brush your teeth, Brush your hair, Eat Breakfast, Put on your clothes." She was teaching us about process and structure. Today as adults, many of us start our day by looking at our calendars and game-planning our list of to do items. This too is a process-driven technique to help us manage our productivity and keep track of what we will accomplish each day.

Have you ever gone back and written down things you did during the day so you could experience the true pleasure of marking it off the list? I do it all the time! I need the satisfaction of seeing my process: write it down, complete the task, and mark the task off the list. Sounds crazy? Well the satisfaction it yields is worth looking a little crazy.

Feed the dog
Go by the bank
Call back XYZ client
Pick up prescription
Breathe
Drop off dry cleaning
Find out the meaning of life.

2. Process is a Creative Endeavor

Study the conditions under which creativity thrives, and process is at the top of the list. I practice this in all my workshop settings with my clients. Imagine for a moment I am teaching my "Conversations on Life Support" workshop, and I tell the group to pair off. They follow my instructions, and I say, "For the next five minutes I want you to have a critical conversation." You will certainly hear crickets in the room because they don't know where to begin the conversation. They have no clearly defined direction, and they flounder.

But when I provide them with a process, their creativity turns on like a faucet. Instead of saying, "Have a critical conversation," I tell them this:

1. I want you to have a five-minute critical conversation. One of you will play the role of manager, and one will play the role of employee.
2. The employee has recently gotten divorced. His team members have complained to you on multiple occasions that he is airing all the dirty details of his divorce with not only the team but with clients.
3. The goal of the conversation is to discuss this issue, hear his point of view, and work together to come up with a solution.

Now we are talking! Providing the process (structure/parameters) for having the conversation allows the duo to be a dynamic duo and have a GREAT conversation.

3. Process is Where Growth Happens

Socrates (old, dead, white guy, born 469 BC in Greece, considered the father of Western philosophy, immortalized in *Bill and Ted's Excellent Adventure*) said this:

The unexamined life is not worth living.

I would like to order a T-shirt, bumper sticker, mouse pad, and coffee cup that says this. My belief system dictates that I never, ever become convinced of my own rightness. I don't have it all figured out. In the case of how humans communicate: Evolution and learning to do better is always an option. You will never have it all figured out either. Never. For those people who are under the false impression that they do, in fact, have it all figured out, there is an inevitable outcome: They become complacent (Again, just ask Kodak).

When I teach a workshop on how to be a stand out public speaker, I advise my students from the beginning on the importance of process. I sell the idea like this: Providing a process does not stunt growth, it encourages it!

> I am going to teach you a process from concept to creation to delivery that I want you to use for your presentation. It may feel a bit formulaic at first, but I will give you room within the process to reveal your personality and what makes you interesting and amazing. If you will do it my way and follow my process something INCREDIBLE is going to happen. Over time, you will know the process from the inside out so that you could do it in your sleep. When you reach that point, you are going to begin to develop your signature style as a speaker, and Tony Robbins will have nothing on you! That is where the growth happens. You develop, you evolve, you move forward.

Think of an Olympic athlete. How do they reach that level of athleticism? Through discipline, structure, and process, that's how. (I used to reference Tiger Woods as my example of using process to be the top athlete in Golf but, he went and lost his mind. If I ever do a workshop on how to completely self destruct he is absolutely back in the rotation.)

In 2008, as the Beijing summer Olympics approached, *Forbes* magazine asked the question "How do Olympians train?". Imagine for a moment that you want to be an Olympic athlete in your favorite event. I pick gymnastics. No ice skating. No track and field. Anyway, just pick an event. Here is what *Forbes* magazine found the best Olympic athletes did to reach their goal:

1. Start four to eight years before the Olympic games to maximize things like lung capacity, heart strength, and lactate tolerance.
2. Plan out a daily training schedule, and be prepared to spend 6 to 10 hours a day training 6 days a week.
3. Hire a team of people to help reach peak performance: A coach, a trainer, a nutritionist, an exercise physiologist, a sports medicine specialist, and a psychologist.
4. Be prepared to be separated from loved ones for long periods of time.

This extreme example illustrates the discipline and structure needed to achieve peak performance in your field. In our lives, the conditions are typically not as extreme as someone going for the Gold, and we don't have to give up everything and maintain a singular focus on our one goal. But...you get the idea. There is always a place for process in our growth plan.

The problem for many people is not agreeing with the theory of process, but finding one that is the right fit for them. I understand.

4. Process is Not a Panacea

I am a big fan of the blog *Eyes on Sales*. The delivery of their email in my inbox today could not have been more timely. Paul McCord- a trainer, educator, and sales expert- is thinking about process too, and this little gem was worth noting here. McCord writes: "Process is a tool for a salesperson just as a paintbrush is a tool for an artist. Put a paintbrush in the hands of an artist with the passion and drive of a Leonardo and it becomes an instrument to create beauty; put it in the hands of someone one who is only looking to make a buck and it is nothing more than a tool used to paint a wall." http://www.eyesonsales.com/author/paul_mccord/

I could not agree more with Mr. McCord. Process is an instrument to be used by those who are looking to make art--whether it is a painting or a life plan. The use of process does not guarantee transformation or growth though and must be accompanied by someone who is willing to do the work.

The Development of What's Your Plan Be?

The remainder of this book is focused on activities to help you find Your Plan Be. These are a series of activities that I have developed over the last fifteen years both in the classroom when I was an instructor, and working with clients in a professional capacity. Each of them serve a specific purpose in helping you answer this one question: What's Your Plan Be?

The activities are meant to be done in the order they are laid out in the chapter, as they build on one another. As you do each activity remember: You can do the activities to find Your Plan Be, but if you want to do it for your organization/business/team/group you certainly can do this as well.

1. Find Your Three Words
2. Identify Your NO NO List
3. Make Peace with Your Lizard Brain
4. Be Your Own Dictionary
5. Get Ready to Break some Rules
6. What do you bring to the table?
7. What's Your Plan Be?
8. Plan To Fail

Before we get started, I want to have what we call in my house a "Come to Jesus." I feel an obligation to be 100% up front with you before you jump in, so bear with me.

There is a strong possibility that you will read this book, do a few of the activities, and find in the after math that this made ZERO difference in your life. Let's face it, the bookshelves at Barnes and Noble are littered with titles similar to this one, promising you that great success and rainbows and unicorns are in your future. The truth is, what you get out of this book is going to be the direct result of what you put into it.

I am certain there are other books/systems/programs out there that will provide you great results in the same way that this process can potentially provide you with great results. The challenge is this: Can you bridge the gap between knowing something and doing it? I read a book on open heart surgery the other day. Would you let me do your open heart surgery? Doubt it. That is my point. Just because you read the book does not mean you can PRACTICE what you learned.

We are a culture of self-help book junkies. We move from one promise to the other and there is a marketplace of millionaires out there who have gotten rich selling you the newest flavor of the month in "dreams come true" land.

I sat down and wrote out the book version of What's Your Plan Be? because I am an educator. It is the core of who I am, and I saw the potential for this book to make a difference for people. But it comes with no money back guarantees or promises that you are going to wake up tomorrow a brand new person.

Before you grab a pen and complete these activities, here is what I will tell you.

1. You will have to be 100% honest with yourself as you move from one activity to the next.
2. Are you ready to get out of your head and do the hard work? FEAR is the number one issue holding people back from finding their Plan Be and putting it into action. If you are too worried about what other people will think, hurting someone's feelings, or looking like a fool, then you are not ready for this program. I am CHALLENGING you to tell your fear to suck it. Yep. That's what I said. You cannot experience growth and transformation when you operate from a place of fear.
3. You cannot fake your way to success. If you are not ready to do the hard work, then you aren't ready. That's just the truth of it.
4. If your dream is to be living someone's else's Plan Be then step away from the book and go get a margarita.
5. Get real about what success means to you. You must, must, must be ready to move away from the idea that material/monetary gain is the meaning of success. I am not Suze Orman, and this is not a book about finances. Piles of Money = Success is not going to be the end game for finding Your Plan Be. This is not

50
WYPB

the kind of book that will get you there. This is a different kind of message.   This is a message that says there is more to life than money. A lot more. I promise.

If you are waiting for me to send you to your room now, I apologize for putting on my mom hat and getting parental. I don't want to sound parental or like you have been in the principal's office, but I did want to be honest and up front with you before we jump into the pool.

If you are still with me (oh lord I hope you are still with me!) then we are ready to start with the first activity--find your three words.

One's vocabulary needs constant
fertilizing or it will die

Evelyn Waugh

ACTIVITY #1:
Find YOUR three words

"Libby, Libby, Libby on the label, label, label."

The power to name something is one of the most awesome powers there is in the world. Think about it. When you are about to become a parent for the first time, how many hours do you labor over thinking of the perfect name for your new son or daughter? I suppose I appreciate this truth more than a lot of people because of my name. I am Libby. Not Elizabeth or Olivia. My name is Libby.

In 1973, there were no other Libby's in my school, neighborhood, or church. Heck, there were not any Libby's anywhere; except for the canned vegetable aisle at the grocery store. I cannot tell you how many times I was taunted by kids and adults (and it still happens to this day) with:

LIBBY, LIBBY, LIBBY
ON THE LABEL, LABEL, LABEL
IF YOU LIKE IT, LIKE IT, LIKE IT
YOU WILL PUT IT ON YOUR TABLE.

I did not know as a young girl that this was a popular commercial on TV before I was born. My neighbor, Chuck Crouch, who was about ten years older than me, would tease me with this song all the time. The first time I heard someone else sing it, my immediate thought was, "Chuck Crouch is telling everyone to sing this to me! He is a terrible, awful person!"

Add to my pain the fact that my two older sister's names are Lisa and Lauren. Are those not beautiful names I ask you? My sister Lauren has always been overly proud of her name, so it only added to my feelings of embarrassment over my unusual name. I vowed when I became a mom that I would not name my children something that they would be taunted by the rest of their lives.

I can tell you now, as I approach my fortieth birthday, that I have come to embrace my unusual name. I have had people tell me on multiple occasions, "But you are Libby! There is no other name for you! You are a Libby!"

Sally Hogshead, speaker and author of *Fascinate,* has a wonderful take on her unusual name. She writes on her website: "Hogshead is a barrel that holds 62 gallons. So what's your name smart ass?" (www.sallyhogshead.com)

I love this! It gives all of us with names that will never make the top-ten baby names list something to celebrate.

The power to name something is one of the most awesome powers there is.

While you may have not gotten to name yourself, in many ways you do have the power to influence how people see you and who they say you are. Who do people say you are?

Within my extended family structure, one of the most enduring stories that gets told about me is how I loved to give performances in the living room of my childhood home. I would stand on the fireplace and grab the pull chain on the fireplace screen usuing it as my microphone. I would sing, dance, and tell stories. I was miserably bad at the singing and dancing part, but the storytelling moments in my performance were something to remember!

"Performer" is most certainly something all of my family and friends would tell you defines me. I have always gravitated toward a microphone. What stories get told about you by family and friends? I would be wiling to bet within these stories lies Your Three Words.

Your Three Words is an activity I use to help you whittle away all the excess and find the heart of who you are in this world. Some people might call it your spiritual gift. When I was still teaching in the classroom and working with students on their presentations, I would ask them, "What three things do you want your audience to remember about your presentation?"

That question is where the activity Your Three Words was born. Outside of the classroom, as I started working with professionals, I began to see a need for coaching people on how to develop their elevator speech.

The elevator speech is a popular networking concept used to communicate to others who you are, what you do, and why it matters in about 45 to 60 seconds. I go to a lot of networking events, as it is a necessary tool for me to meet new people and forge new relationships. So there I am, at said networking event, and I need to introduce myself in a way that will CAPTIVATE my listener. What do I say?

I teach public speaking workshops to professionals across many different industries, and I have found that the 45-to-60 second presentation of self and business is one of the MOST challenging assignments I present them. They can almost always go into a long and drawn out overview of their organization, their product, and their service, but when I say "now say all that in four sentences," they fall apart.

Many people's elevator speech suffers from the Charlie Brown Teacher Syndrome.

The Charlie Brown Phone Elevator Speech looks like this: "Hello, my name is Libby Spears with Bravo communications and consulting and my company works with you to maximize your communication skills in all contexts from public speaking to leadership and management to interpersonal skills development in order to grow your business wonh wonh wonh wonh wonh."

Right? You all remember when the teacher would call Charlie Brown's house--well all too often our elevator speech sounds exactly like that. Part of the reason is because there is a lack of simplicity in our message.

Your goal is to rise about the Charlie Brown phone syndrome by finding Your Three Words and simplifying your message.

Simplicity is a concept that is lost on many people. The ability to achieve simplicity is something to toil over because it gets to the heart of who you are and why it matters (for an excellent and more in depth look at simplicity see *Made to Stick* by Chip and Dan Heath). The example I use to illustrate this point is what I call The Steven Spielberg principle. The Steven Spielberg principle is this:

Of all the directors in the history of directors (in my opinion) Steven Spielberg is the best. Some of my favorite movies of all time, including *ET, The Color Purple,* and *Indiana Jones,* come from the genius direction of Mr. Spielberg. But as good as he is, and really does he have any equal I ask you, he still has an EDITOR on all his films.

Editing of a film is so important you can win an Oscar for it (the winners are usually the ones you fast forward through on TiVo or go to the Kitchen to get a snack during their acceptance speech--yeah those guys).

If you have ever bought a DVD of your favorite movie, you may have noticed that some releases have the director's cut. The director's cut is usually less cohesive and includes footage that landed on the editing room floor in final edits. A few years ago I saw the director's cut of two of my favorite movies: *Dances with Wolves* and *Tombstone.* I was not happy! I did not like the director's cut at all, and it was a learning moment for me--I began to appreciate just how important editing is. A truly great editor knows how to get to the heart of the story. A great editor is a master of simplicity.

If you are thinking like Mr. Spielberg, you recognize that being a stand out director requires you to have a stand out editor.

Now you understand the purpose of the activity as well as the benefits to finding Your Three Words. But where do you find Your Three Words? Answer the following questions to get you thinking about your own unique combination of three words.

1. When you volunteer your time, what kinds of roles do you typically play?

2. When was the last time you completed a task and thought to yourself "I am truly a bad ass!"?

3. What job would you do for free because you enjoy it that much?

4. What were your favorite games to play when you were a kid?

5. What kinds of stories do your family and friends tell about you?

6. How would the following people describe you? (and if you don't know then ask them...)

PERSON	THEY WOULD DESCRIBE ME AS:
Spouse/Significant Other	
Parents	
Siblings	
Children	
Best Friend	
Boss	
Co-Worker	
Clients	

After you have answered these questions, look for patterns and begin to name qualities/characteristics that describe you. If you need help with finding the right word, see the following page for inspiration.

Take a blank piece of paper and using the words on the following two pages as inspiration, brainstorm about 15 words that you think are descriptive of you.

Alleviate	Access	Acknowledge	Ascertain	Amplify	Align
Bestow	Believe	Build	Bridge	Bank	Brighten
Bounty	Brand	Become	Call	Coach	Confer
Collect	Compose	Conceive	Conquer	Critique	Connect
Collaborate	Create	Confirm	Condition	Clean	Compete
Discover	Defend	Distill	Direct	Define	Defy
Drive	Dream	Determine	Disconnect	Disarm	Dissect
Delve	Drum-up	Decide	Embrace	Enjoy	Elaborate
Empower	Explore	Engage	Employ	Foster	Finalize
Find	Finish	Fish	Forge	Free	Formalize
Finesse	Heal	Harness	Hope	Identify	Impress
Illuminate	Isolate	Improvise	Launch	Lead	Learn
Liberate	Listen	List	Laugh	Manifest	Mentor
Measure	Motivate	Move	Manage	Materialize	Message
Nurture	Notice	Negotiate	Offer	Order	Organize
Officiate	Oversee	Play	Promote	Pursue	Provide
Reclaim	Reduce	Realize	Relate	Relax	Restore
Satisfy	Strong	Survive	Strive	Satisfy	Surrender
Sustain	Support	Save	Spend	Strengthen	Speak
Team	Touch	Translate	Tell	Teach	Trend
Transform	Understand	Undo	Unburden	Utilize	Verbal
Value	Venture	Wonder	Wish	Work	Worship
Walk	Whisper	Walk	Widen		

*Help me grow my list! Share YOUR three words at www.facebook.com/bravocc

The list of words above are fairly "vanilla" aren't they? I think that in finding Your Three Words, you need to consider the value of adding a word/phrase that is unusual and provokes interest for your third word. Below, in no particular order, are a few interesting words to get you thinking.

Smarty Pants	Rabble Rouser	Pot Stirrer	Rule Breaker	Fun Maker	Change Agent
Evangelist	Cheerleader	Zookeeper	Cat Herder	Trend maker	Taste Maker
Fashion Don't	Fierce	Feisty	Nerd	Ninja	Geek
Tour Guide	Director of Fun	Grammar Police	Talent Spotter	Social Sally	Welcome Wagon
Entertainer	Storyteller	Maverick	Warrior	Navigator	Scalawag

*Avoid the word Guru in choosing your three words. It is an overused word and people tend to dismiss it now because the word has become nothing more than a cliche.
*Nerd, Ninja, and Geek also run the risk of becoming cliched as well. Pay attention, and if you see these used everywhere then you might want to back away from the word!

We are ready to begin the process of narrowing down your three words.

1. Look at your list and mark off words that are simply a repeat of another word on the list.

2. Mark off words that are not VERY Descriptive of you. For example, if you wrote the word kind, take it off the list! KIND is nebulous. It doesn't really tell me anything about you.

3. Go online and use a thesaurus and find similar words if you need to find "kissing cousins" to the words you like best. Would one of these words be a better fit for you?

4. Sit for a moment and reflect on the words that remain. Take your pen and circle the three that best describe how you see yourself. Remember--these are the words that represent the unique combination of qualities and characteristics about you.

Once you have determined Your Three Words, you want to arrange them.
1. Your first word should be that thing that is in your DNA. You can't not do it. For me it is educate. I can't not teach and I know it is in my DNA. I have known this since I was a little girl and had a big chalkboard in my room along with lesson plans I had written for my imaginary classroom of kids.

2. Your second word should challenge us a little bit. Choose a word that might be a surprising way to capture your talent. My second word is liberate. You will read later why I chose this word.

3. Your third word should be that quality that is the perfect compliment to the first two words and also not something you always find with other people who may do what you do or have the same talent you do. Say for example that you have a strategic mind for numbers. Let's also say that you really like people and enjoy socializing. These are qualities you don't always find in other people who are "numbers people." In fact they often get a bad rap because they are good with numbers but bad with people (reminds me of some of my math teachers). In this case, your three words might be:

Strategic | Number-cruncher | Socializer
(yeah I am ok with compound words!)

If your three words would be better articulated as three phrases then go for it. I am not going to show up at your door and tell you that you have failed in life because you didn't do the activity as three words. Here is an example:

> "I work with small business owners to **ALIGN** their product/service with a specific user group's needs | I **STRATEGIZE** with my client ways to stand out in the marketplace | I **LAUNCH** these ideas in real and meaningful ways for my client."

Now, take the three key words:
ALIGN | STRATEGIZE | LAUNCH

Bam! You have Your Three Words! (Clever huh?)

What I have described is a great marketing person, but doesn't it mean so much more when I use these three words to tell you who I am versus, "I am in marketing"? Because what does it mean to actually "market"? What an abstract term that is! And it means so many different things to people. With these three words, I have defined what someone in marketing does. It is interesting and intriguing and makes me want to know more about this person.

When you find Your Three Words, be ready to provide an anecdote to SHOW me how these three words work in practice. Tell me about a time you did these three things and then show the benefit.

Consider the example on the next page of a traditional business card. One has the expected title of CEO, and the other has My Three Words. Which compels you more? Which do you find more interesting? Which one makes you want to turn over the business card and learn more about what I do?

Before you decide on your three words a few things to note:

1. Don't pick a word because Plan A says you are expected to be those things (women are supposed to be nurturing for example).

2. Don't choose a word because it is how people have always labeled you, but does not speak to the truth of who you are.

3. Don't choose words that are who you wish you were but you aren't. Look, I wish one of my core strengths was organization. But it is not. And it never will be. It would be wrong for me to present myself to the world as a master organizer when I am not.

4. You are not going to be expected to tattoo these three words on your arm. I am not asking you to make a lifetime commitment with a ceremony officiated by a priest. In fact, I am well aware that in a few years you may need to circle back around to this activity because you have changed, your passions have changed, etc.

5. Do not, under any circumstance, diminish or dismiss Your Three Words. I had someone tell me recently that her spiritual gift was being a hostess. Before I could get out, "Oh that is a wonderful gift to share with the world!" she was telling me the 42 reasons no one cared about someone who was good at hostessing. So I slapped her. No I didn't slap her. But I wanted to.

When you find and share Your Three Words, you are giving the world the opportunity to let you be more of who you are. I have seen with my own eyes new adventures present themselves to people when they take the time to do this activity.

If you have found Your Three Words, grab a Post It note and write them down! Put Your Three Words on your computer, your fridge, your bathroom mirror, and SHARE it with other people. Do it. Do it right now.

Finding the hree words that encapsulate who you are gives you a reference point for making decisions in your personal and professional life. I spoke at a women's lunch a few years ago about finding your Plan Be and a woman did not want to participate in the Your Three Words activity. When I looked down at her sheet of paper she had written:

"I am me."

I challenged her (go figure).

"But what are your three words?" I asked her.

"Well I don't want to be defined, so I just wrote 'I am me'," she responded.

What I wanted to say to her was, "whatever," and move on, but I calmly explained:

"Telling another person who you are allows them to see your unique set of strengths. It allows them to plug you in to the right place. And let's be honest here--none of us are undefinable."

We could all stand to do a little self-defining (and if you don't define yourself someone else might do it for you and do you really trust someone else to pick YOUR three words?).

"Yes," I wanted to tell this buzz killer, "I get you are so amazingly unique that the English language simply can't capture your essence, but let's try shall we?"

Take My Three Words:
educator | liberator | entertainer

It took me some time to arrive at these three words. After all, there are so many to choose from! But these three words define me. At my core I am an educator. I am always teaching. As a kid what I loved to play the most was teacher.

I believe your first word should be that thing that is in your D.N.A. I can't not teach. I have always been teaching, and it is truly the word I would use to describe myself. I am passionate about teaching. It gets me high.

My second word, liberator, was chosen to help explain what I do for a living in more depth. When a client hires me, my job is to identify the communication strategies used by an individual or an organization that are holding them back from their success, and liberate them from those bad habits. Then we replace them with new ways of telling their story.

Finally, I am an entertainer. As the youngest of three girls, I think I come by this naturally. I love telling stories, making people laugh, and having a good time.

These are My Three Words. These three words have power. They tell people who I am and who I am not. And they serve as a reminder to myself of who I am. One fringe benefit I found later is that these three words also helped me to identify the people who get me and those who don't get me.

Consider my business card. Instead of "CEO," "President," or "Master of the Universe," my business card simply says: educator, liberator, entertainer.

I like to mail my parents my marketing materials, so I threw a card in the mail to them to get their rave reviews (because I expected nothing less).

Well that is not the reaction I got.

On the phone with my mom I asked, "Did you get my new business card?"

She responded, "Yes and your dad wants to get on the phone."

This was funny. Here I was a grown woman with a mortgage and kids of my own, and suddenly I had that feeling that I was about to get in trouble.

My mom: "Your dad and I have some concerns about your new business card."

Me: "Excuse me?"

Mom: "It doesn't say anywhere on there that you are CEO, President, or Owner."

Me: "Mom, Bravo cc consists of two people, so I don't think that those titles are really applicable here."

Mom: "Well these three words you have on there--I just think people are going to get the wrong idea bout you."

Me: "Do tell."

Mom: "Well take liberator for example. If a man saw that he would think that means you are into women's lib. He will think you are a feminist."

Me: "I am a feminist."

Mom: "And entertainer. That makes me think of a pole dancer or a stripper."

Me: "So what you are saying is that someone looking at my card will interpret it to mean that I am teacher who hates men, doesn't wear a bra, and dances on a pole?"

Mom: "Yes."

My dad agreed by not saying anything at all. That is how he agrees.

Do my parents not get me? On some level I think they don't. I blame our generational differences for this lack of understanding. My mom, for example, grew up professionally in a generation that had very, very, very different rules for women in the workplace as well as an industry (banking) that is still very conservative.

People who respond to my three words are the people I want to work with.

I tell people, "I am a teacher, not a preacher." I don't have time to convert the masses. I want to work with people who get it on some level but need help from someone like me to guide them on how to implement new ideas, new practices, and new ways of doing things.

People who respond to my three words are the people I want to work with. I don't have to bust my behind to convince them that I know what I am talking about. They get it, and they need and want my help.

Your Three Words need to go somewhere that you will see them and you can remind and reinforce who you are, and what you are working toward for yourself. When an opportunity comes your way, use your three words to measure if it makes sense for you. Does this opportunity allow you to be more of who you are, or does it make you refocus on something that really doesn't play to your strengths?

You don't need a business card, fancy title, or J-O-B for this activity to have meaning. Your Three Words apply to all aspects of your life. If you are volunteering for an organization, for example, use Your Three Words to offer the organization your greatest strengths. At home, and in your relationships with your family, use your three words to remind one another of what you bring to the family.

Let me synthesize the value of this activity before moving to the next activity. Here is WHY Your Three Words is a valuable activity.

1. If you don't define yourself, someone else will. Do you want to let someone else decide who you are? Me either.
2. Finding Your Three Words gives you a reference point for making decisions. When presented with an opportunity you can ask yourself "Will saying yes to this help me be more of who I am?"
3. There is beauty in simplicity. Simplifying who you are in just three words is far more effective than a long drawn out explanation. When you meet me for the first time and ask, "What do you do?" and I tell you, "I am an educator, I liberate my

clients from dead end practices, and I am an entertainer," you are going to have much better sense of what I do than if I said, "I am a consultant."

4. Your Three Words will allow you to identify the people who get you and those who don't get you. If you have to spend a lot of time trying to explain/justify Your Three Words to someone else, there is a strong likelihood that they don't understand you and what makes you fantastic.

5. Your three words capture your best talents. By naming your talents in three words you tell yourself and the world, "This is what I offer the world!"

6. It allows you to tell people where to plug you in. Take a volunteer role for example. When you can tell the group, "Here is where you can make the most of my volunteer efforts," the group will be more successful in the long run.

The final step in this activity is to determine what to do with these three words. I would like to suggest a trip to the tattoo parlor. No? Ok. Here a few a things to do instead.

1. Grab some Post It notes and write down Your Three Words. Next, stick the Post It note in three places where you will be reminded that this is who you are and who you want to be more of. I suggest your bathroom mirror, your desktop/ laptop, and your fridge.

2. Consider using Your Three Words on your next order of business cards. I think it is wonderful if you are the President, CEO, Director of your department, etc. Titles are nice, but they say very little about who we are as people. Your title tells the world where you fit in to the organizational structure, but Your Three Words tell the world what it will be like to work with you. I like that idea. You don't have to get rid of the title on your business card, because if your mom is like my mom, she won't like that one little bit. But perhaps you can add Your Three Words? Give it a try and see what happens.

3. While you are at it, start using Your Three Words in your marketing materials. This is a great idea for small business owners who are working to develop their brand awareness. In the same way that you determined Your Three Words, take the time to do the same activity for your organization/business. The name of the game in today's marketplace is to capture the short attention span of your client/ customer base + differentiate yourself from the rest of the crowd. I believe this activity does just that.

4. When you are at a networking event and have the opportunity to introduce yourself and tell someone who you are, what you do, and why it matters--Your Three Words are a fantastic way to achieve this. Here is an example.

"Hi I am Libby Spears and I own my own consulting adventure called Bravo cc. I am sure you have sat through some pretty awful presentations. I work with organizations (professionals) much like yourself to **EDUCATE** you on how to do better presentations, **LIBERATE** you from the Death by Power Point Business Presentation model and **ENTERTAIN** you in the process because when I work, I like to have fun and I know you do too."

Kabam!

5. As you practice using your three words, be prepared to connect the dots between the three words and illustrate how unique this combination is! You won't find it anywhere else. In the instance of my three words, my combination is interesting because most educators are not typically entertainers too. I tell everyone, "I can teach you better than anyone you will meet, and you will have fun doing it!"

You are on your way to finding and defining Your Plan Be with this activity.
Let's move forward!

*Notice in the above example I don't talk about a distant and far off "them," and instead I use "you" to discuss my client. This creates a far better impression and subtly I am suggesting to the person I have just met that we will work together. Brilliant? Yes.

*You will also notice I don't use any tired catch phrases like "transparency," "stakeholder," "think outside the box," "deep dive," etc to talk about what I do. Nothing makes me tune out faster than when a person's pitch goes into corporate head nod language.

BLOG EXTRA!
Meet Kronda Thimesch

I recently emceed a women's conference. In preparation for the event, I reached out to the conference sponsors who would be given a sixty second spotlight at the conference to talk about their business. I encouraged these women to find their three words and use them to structure their presentation. Below I share the contribution from Kronda Thimesch, owner of Green Meadows Landscaping.

What three words best describe me? Knowing that these three words were going to be given to an entire Women's Conference almost made me re-think my session sponsorship! That was not listed in the fine print. I found the process of coming up with words that would be spoken out loud to others an uncomfortable process. I agonized over it for days and solicited the help of good friends. The results were surprisingly liberating as it allowed me to see both strengths and weaknesses in those words. This activity has given me the courage to move forward, and grace to know I won't always do it perfectly.

Three Words that best describe Kronda Thimesch:
Loyal – "all in." Once I begin something I finish regardless of difficulties or conflict (which does make me careful in committing to a project).
Compassionate – Love for those who need encouragement, both physically and spiritually. I want to make a difference in the life of another person whether I am recognized for it or not.
Teachable – I want to know more! How can I do it better, find another creative solution to this problem, or study something to learn how to make it work? Learning to be a better mom, business woman and leader, spiritually in my walk with the Lord. I want to be known as a life long learner.

Three Words that best describe Green Meadows Landscaping
So fun to think about because I love the people I work with, and all that they bring in their creative work for our clients. The culture of Green Meadows is permeated by these three words. Not just Jeff & Kronda, but each and every person who works for Green Meadows Landscaping.
Integrity – The honestly of each employee and the trust that we have in them allows us to run a company that has core values of honesty and truthfulness. We mean what we say and we do it. Providing work visas for our employees, background checks, taxes, payroll, estimates, to projects completed for clients. We want to be above reproach in everything we do.
Faithful – Our employees define our company. They have worked for us for years, and bring their best each and every day. We have employees who often do things that others would not want to do, even for a paycheck.
Creative– We have a creative team that transforms dysfunctional spaces into living areas that are useful to you and your family. Not what is best for me, but what works best for you and your needs.

BLOG EXTRA!
The High Cost of Self Delusion

I am about half way through "*What Got you Here Won't Get You There*" by Marshall Goldsmith, a pretty good read on how to break some of our worst habits to reach our full potential. There is not, so far, anything revolutionary in his list of bad habits that hold us back, but I am always a fan of repetition to reinforce some of those hard learned lessons. I have paused to put down here a great thought from this very book, found on p. 134.

"Your flaws at work don't vanish when you walk through the front door at home."

that is worth typing again:

"YOUR FLAWS AT WORK DON'T VANISH WHEN YOU WALK THROUGH THE FRONT DOOR AT HOME."

I hear people I work with tell me all the time "I am different outside of the work place," and honestly, I have a pretty tough time believing them. The area I struggle most with in my life is organization. I know that about me. It shows up in my personal life and my business life. I don't magically become an organizational guru when I am working.

Goldsmith tells of a Gordon Gekko like character he worked with who was VERY successful financially, but a disaster in his professional relationships. Essentially everyone he worked with hated the man. When Goldsmith sat down with him to address this flaw, the guy's response to him was, "Oh that is just me at work, I don't act like that at home." So Goldsmith got his wife on the phone who literally burst out laughing at her husbands self-delusional statement. I think the word she used was "jerk" to describe him at home. Just for good measure, Goldsmith got his kids on the phone too. And they corroborated her story. OUCH!

My point? Pay attention to the complaints you receive at home, and there is a good chance that those are the very qualities that are holding you back not just in your personal relationships but in your professional relationships too. Maya Angelou once said "When people show you who they are, believe them." I would add to that--if they show you to be one thing at work, they are likely the same way at home--and vice versa.

Take a week and write down all the comments that people make about you. Even the comments your kids make. Write down the good with the bad. At the end of the week, sit down and see if any patterns emerge from these "passing remarks." Then make a plan to do better.

Learn to say no.
It will be of more use to you than to
be able to read Latin.

Charles H. Spurgeon

ACTIVITY #2:
Identify Your NO-NO List

When my youngest daughter Trinity was in kindergarten, she joined a Girl Scout troop. I did not do Girl Scout's when I was a kid (I did Camp Fire Girls). When she became a Girl Scout, I was excited because it would help forge new friendships, and I like what Girl Scouts stands for. It was all good.

Except for one thing. You see, I didn't read the fine print, and when your daughter signs up for Girl Scouts, you sign up for Girl Scouts (the people who know me really well are laughing right now because they know where this is headed). Every year, the Girl Scouts hit the streets and start selling those addictive Girl Scout cookies. I love to eat cookies. If there was a job that needed to be filled by a Girl Scout mom to eat cookies, I would have signed up for that responsibility in a heart beat. Turns out, they didn't have a need for a mom to eat cookies, but the troop did need a mom to be what is affectionately known as "The Cookie Mom."

The Cookie Mom oversees all cookie sales. She picks up cookies, stores them at her house until they are distributed, and collects money from the little girl's Thin-Mint-Stained hands at the end of the cookie sales season. The first two or three years Trinity was a Girl Scout, a mom from our troop always volunteered happily to be The Cookie Mom. This was a huge relief, but I knew that eventually all eyes were going to land on me, and the expectation would be crystal clear: It was my turn to be The Cookie Mom.

The troop leader also happens to be a good friend, and she is, without a doubt, put on this earth to be a Girl Scout Troop Mom. Shelley is a natural leader, and I am starting to suspect she is also a vampire because I don't think she ever sleeps. She is, in short, amazing. I knew that the day was coming where we would have to address the fact that I was not stepping up and volunteering to be The Cookie Mom, so I began to plan how I would explain the situation to her.

I invoked what good, Southern women have been saying for hundreds of years. No--not "bless your heart"--but that is one of my favorites too.

I told Shelley, "Cookie Mom is not my spiritual gift."

And it isn't. I wasn't feeding her a line of B.S. It was the truth. I have a rule that I try to follow when it comes to volunteering: I don't volunteer for things that involve me handling other people's money. I heard a story from someone years ago about a woman who was on her way to make a deposit of a great deal of cash from a fundraiser. The deposit was in her purse. As luck would have it, she needed gas on the way to the bank.

She stopped. Filled up. Drove away.

And her purse was on the trunk of the car. With the cash.

That story has haunted me for years because it sounds so very much like something I would do. I can SEE this happening, in slow motion, and I wonder if that poor woman is now living in some remote village in a far away country because of the embarrassment of such a bone headed move.

Handling money that belongs to other people is on my No-No list.

A lot of people struggle with saying the word NO, so I coach them to say, "That's not my spiritual gift." There is a follow up to that sentence though. You must then be ready to say, "This is my spiritual gift, and when there is a need for it, I am your girl/guy for the job."

In the case of the Girl Scouts, I would be willing to bet that Shelley would tell you I never really plugged in my spiritual gift to our troop. Don't tell anyone, but I am not a kid person. Or a camping person. Or a craft person. What I am trying to tell you is that I sucked as a Girl Scout Mom. I am happy to report though that my pantry has boxes of Girl Scout cookies in it, and Shelley and I are still very good friends.

What is on your No-No list?

Perhaps it will help you if I define what kinds of things should go on a No-No list. A No-No list includes those things that you choose not to do in life because it does not make the world a better place. In the same way that you have spiritual gifts, there are also things that are not your spiritual gift.

Here is the kicker though: If you put something on the No-No list will it hurt you personally or professionally? If you choose to put an item on the No-No list is there someone else out there in your life who has this same item on their spiritual gift list and you can find ways to help each other be more of what you are?

If you are going to put something on your No-No list, you must be ready to have a plan to fill this gap or be willing to suffer the consequence. If there is one thing I have learned in building my business it is this simple truth: When you define those things you don't want to do, find someone else who can fill the gap (because it is their gift), and work harder at your spiritual gifts, the world will be a better place.

What that means then is I spend money for someone to do the things on my No-No list, which then frees me up to do what I am great at....and make more money. This makes sense, and yet I see professionals, small business owners, and new entrepreneurs trying to do things that should be on their No-No list because they are living out of fear. They are afraid to spend the money on someone who can do it right (design that new business card, handle the books, process payroll, build a website), and they end up doing work that is sub-par and limits their growth.

Here is my No-No list to give you an idea of how to get started on your own list.

Libby's NO-No List	IS THERE A CONSEQUENCE TO PUTTING THIS ON MY LIST?	IS THERE SOMEONE I KNOW WHO THIS IS THEIR GIFT?
Don't handle other people's money.	NO. I rarely am in a position to have to handle money that does not belong to me!	I work with a number of committees and there always seems to be a person who gravitates to this role. Thank the lord!
Paperwork, filing, filling out forms, etc.	YES! Part of running a business means paperwork. That means I have to be willing to spend the money on an assistant to do these things, so I can do the things I am good at.	Lara my assistant is great at keeping me caught up on administrative items.
Editing my work.	When my work is not 100% perfect it impacts my credibility. But I hate editing. That means I have to be willing to pay someone to put their eyes on my work to catch edits.	Melissa Cox. She is a great editor, and we have a fantastic working relationship where I share my gifts with her in exchange for her gifts. It's a win/win!
House Keeping: Weekly Cleaning.	I like to live in a clean and orderly home, so yes there is a consequence to me not taking care of this task. I work harder at the things I am good at, so that I can pay someone to clean my house.	Rosie! She is a successful business owner and takes good care of my house. I am so blessed to have her clean my house.
Volunteering for things that involve school-aged kids.	If I worry about what other moms think about me, then there is a potential consequence because I will be judged. I have learned though to not worry about trying to live up to some idea of what a mom is supposed to do (Plan A). Now that my girls are getting older, it is less of an issue too.	I have many, many friends who are great in these kinds of situations.

Now you are ready to make your No-No list. Here is a blank form for you to work with.

My NO-No List	IS THERE A CONSEQUENCE TO PUTTING THIS ON MY LIST?	IS THERE SOMEONE I KNOW WHO THIS IS THEIR GIFT?

Learning to say no to things takes courage. When you say "Yes" to everything you start to feel like a doormat. I am certain there is no one who lays in bed at night, and thinks, "I want to Be a doormat."

Take another look at your No-No list. Before we move to the next activity think about your relationships, your life, and your to-do list. Where are THREE places you want to say No?

1.

2.

3.

Beginning here with THREE things you will say no to is a good start. And if saying no just doesn't feel right, that's OK. You can say:

"No thank you."

Take the above page, laminate it, punch a hole in the top of the page and wear it like a necklace. Doesn't match your outfit? OK, no problem. Instead, grab a Post It note and write down the THREE things you are going to say no to and put it somewhere that you will be reminded of this today, tomorrow, and in the future.

Here are the things I say no to:

1. Will you be homeroom mom? No
2. Can you teach a workshop on time management? No
3. Will you lead the prayer at our family Thanksgiving this year? No (I am not a public prayer kind of person.)
4. Would you like to go camping with us? No
5. Will you be cookie mom? No
6. Would you like to go on the student trip and ride on a bus with fifty screaming kids for eight hours both ways? No.

I have said no a lot of times, and I am here to report it did not kill me. I say yes a lot too, but when I say yes, it is to things that play to my strengths. Understand that as you take control of your own Plan Be, you have to say no less because you come into a conversation, relationship, or group ready to say, "These are the things I do really, really well." This strategy makes life so much easier because people don't have to guess what you are great at doing!

Before we move on to the next activity, let me address my fellow smarty-pants reading this. I know you. I know how your mind works because my mind works the same way. With that being said, making a No-No list does not mean you will stop doing anything you don't want to do or does not play to your strengths because it's on the list.

I HATE going to the grocery store, but there are times that it must be done. My kids have gotta eat. I have gotta eat. My husband has gotta eat. I equally detest doing laundry. But wearing dirty clothes is not good form, so of course the laundry must be done. Now, could I stop doing these things? Yes--when I work harder at the things that play to my personal strengths, I am more successful professionally. More success equals more money and more money gives me options. I could pay someone to shop for my groceries and do my laundry, and I won't lie--I have paid someone to do my laundry for me many times.

The No-No list is not designed to create a life where you do everything you love all the time and avoid the things you don't like to do because they are on the list. Au contraire. The point of the No-No list is to help you identify the things that you have a choice to do or not do and learn to say no to them. I don't have to be homeroom mom, but for years I signed up to do it. Why? Because I was trying to prove something to some nameless, faceless person who might judge my worthiness as a mom. I was trying to be something I was not. But here is the problem: When we masquerade as something we are not, we take up real space for someone to fill this role and do it superbly because it is, in fact, their spiritual gift.

By taking the time to build your own No-No list, you will be inspired to ask other people what is on their No-No list. When we give people permission to tell us what they hate doing, they will learn to become comfortable with saying No and learn to lean in to their strengths.

You have found Your Three Words + created your No-No list. You are headed in the right direction! The next step in this journey is to make peace with your Lizard brain.

Nurture your mind with great thoughts, for you will never go any higher than you think.

Benjamin Disraeli

ACTIVITY #3:
Make Peace with Your Lizard Brain

Ten years ago I was asked to deliver the keynote at a faculty colloquium at a community college in Dallas. I was excited. This was one of my first "gigs" as a speaker, and I spent a lot of time planning and preparing my 45-minute presentation. The topic was how to create immediacy in the classroom starting on the first day of class.

When I arrived at the venue, the room was packed with faculty and administrators. The president of the college was scheduled to speak before me to kick things off for the new semester. The organizer of the event told me the president would speak about ten to fifteen minutes and then she would come up and introduce me. Great!

WHAT DOES YOUR LIZARD BRAIN SAY TO YOU BEFORE AND DURING A PRESENTATION?

I took a seat in the front row and prepared to listen to the president. She started her presentation, and for the first ten minutes I was focused on her message. At fifteen minutes she was still speaking, and in my own head I was processing thoughts like, "It doesn't feel like she is about to wrap things up does it?" As I began to tick off the minutes, I was becoming increasingly uncomfortable.

My Lizard brain started to kick in to overdrive.

Your Lizard brain is that voice in your head that does not have your best interests at heart and loves to come out when you are in a stressed state. The concept of the Lizard brain crossed my path a few years ago when I became a dedicated follower of Seth Godin. On Seth's website, he writes, "The Lizard is a physical part of your brain, the pre-historic lump near the brain stem that is responsible for fear and rage and reproductive drive." (http://sethgodin.typepad.com/seths_blog/2010/01/quieting-the-lizard-brain.html)

"Oh that Lizard brain. Yeah I know her. I have even named her. Strangely, her voice sounds a lot like my third grade teacher..."

So I am sitting in my chair, watching the president go well beyond her ten to fifteen minute time allotment when the event organizer comes and whispers in my ear, "Do you think you can do your presentation in thirty minutes?" Shave off fifteen minutes of my pre-planned presentation? No problem. Sounds good. Ideal. No worries.

I began thinking in my own head how I could edit my presentation down to thirty minutes while the president just kept on a talkin'. And talkin'. And talkin' some more. But at this point, I was no longer listening to her because my Lizard brain was blasting her loud, obnoxious, and absurd statements to me.

"You are going to suck!" she told me.

"There is no way in the world you can get this down to thirty minutes and it make sense. What a joke."

"Why did they even hire you to do this anyway? You are kidding yourself. They aren't going to listen to you. They won't care about what you say. What a waste."

As my Lizard brain was busy performing her one woman, Broadway-worthy show, the event organizer materialized beside me, again. "Um....," she said nervously. "Yeah this is not working out the way we planned. I am really sorry. I don't know why she is not finishing up. I am going to need you speak for just twenty minutes. Can you do that?"

"Yep," I said.

As the event organizer walked away, my Lizard brain was saying to me, "This is going to be a career ending day for you sister. Get ready to nose dive straight into the side of a professional cliff."

I am here now, so you can see that the story had an ending where I didn't die or pursue a new career path. How did I handle my Lizard brain in that moment? I will come back to that later, but first let's talk about your Lizard brain.

Everyone has a Lizard brain. I have a Lizard brain. You have a Lizard brain. Unchecked, it can become a tyrannical dictator of your life and 99.9% of the time it does not have your best interests at heart. Like any growth or transformation program, acknowledging the problem is the first step in the right direction. To do that, I want you to say the following out loud:

Well hello there Lizard brain.
It's time for us to have a come to Jesus.

Your Lizard brain is going to do all sorts of sneaky and seductive things to convince you that he/she is your friend and not your foe. Your Lizard brain is going to lie to you, cry to you, and bargain with you to let it continue to have input into your decisions. But you are moving on.

Now that you have said hello to your Lizard brain, let's begin to understand WHY that part of your brain is so powerful.

All of us experience stress in our personal and professional lives, and it is in these moments where our Lizard brain comes out and takes over the show. Getting a handle on stress begins with understanding what is happening when we are in a state of stress.

You have a basic stress response style given the context and the relationship. When stressed, your internal mechanisms kick in and tell you to engage in fight or flight behaviors. Those of us who have a high FIGHT response (me!) respond differently than those who have a high FLIGHT response (Run Forest Run!) style, but interestingly enough, the physiological and biochemical responses for both are very similar.

Taking back your decision making power from your Lizard brain in these moments begins with recognizing what is happening to you before your Lizard brain kicks in and starts making your decisions for you.

Imagine for a moment that you are in a stressful situation: It's Friday afternoon at work and your son has a 6:00pm baseball practice that was scheduled at the last minute. You are getting all your ducks in a row to get out the door by 5:00 when your boss asks if you can come by her office for a minute. You step in to her office and she says, "Could you stay late today? I just got a call from XYZ client and they need the LMNOP Report today instead of Monday."

You are stressed. You are angry. You are frustrated.

Before you pay attention to your Lizard brain, stop for a moment and think about your body. What is it doing?

Those of us with high FIGHT stress responses and those with high FLIGHT stress responses will exhibit the following:

FIGHT!

Heavy Breathing, Blood Pressure Goes Up, Pupils Dilate, Jaw Clenched, Heart is racing, Agitated, Digestion stops, Saliva is not produced, Blood Rushes to arms and legs to prepare for fight, Brain does not process thoughts easily because all the blood flow has left for other parts of your body.

FLIGHT!

Heavy Breathing, Blood Pressure Goes Up, Pupils Dilate, Heart is racing, Agitated, Digestion stops, Saliva is not produced, Blood Rushes to arms and legs to prepare to flee, Brain does not process thoughts easily because all the blood flow has left to allow your body to run away.

Whether you have a higher tendency to fight or flee, many of the same things are happening to your body. These responses are your body's way of preparing you to kick someone's behind or get to stepping and run, run, run. As you can see, both of these responses in the modern world rarely do us any good. Yes, if you are running away from a bear then you need to be ready to run like the wind. If you are challenged by an invading clan of people then you need to be ready to fight.

When is the last time you stared down a bear or an invading clan? Never? Me too.

But here is the problem, your brain and your bodily responses to stress have evolved over thousands and thousands of years, and in today's modern world--when we are stressed, our brain and body respond the same way it did when our pre-civilized ancestors reacted when they were threatened.

It is in these moments that our Lizard brain becomes incredibly powerful.

Wow!

When the flight/flight response is triggered over **1,400 different physiological and biochemical responses** are in play!

Take a moment and consider yourself in different scenarios that are stressful and if you tend to fight or flee. To give you an idea, let me start with my own examples.

STRESSED!	FIGHT OR FLIGHT?	WHAT THAT LOOKS LIKE FOR ME:
Pulled over by a police officer	FIGHT	My mind starts racing, I "bow" up with my body, lean forward, heart is pounding, very defensive non-verbally.
"Called Out" in a public setting	My response is very context and relationship driven in these situations. If it is a personal relationship like family or friends my response is FLIGHT!	VERY emotional. Tears start to flow, my voice shakes, my body shakes, and I can't get my thoughts straight. Heart is beating fast. Very fast.
There is too much going on at one time and I am overwhelmed by it all	FLIGHT!	When I am overwhelmed by too many things going on at one time and I can't get a handle on it, I feel powerless and weak and I shut down. I will retreat, go somewhere alone, and not be in contact with anyone. I tend to have a lot of head talk where my mind is racing, and I can't calm myself down easily.

Now it is your turn to identify your fight and flight tendencies. Take a moment and reflect on your past stressful experiences, and note the times when you were ready to put on the boxing gloves or lace up your sneakers and head for the door.

STRESSED!	FIGHT OR FLIGHT?	WHAT THAT LOOKS LIKE FOR ME:

You are likely having a laugh over my first example with the police officer pulling me over. I have had to work HARD on this one over the years because it is never a good idea to get mouthy with a police officer. I am still not 100% sure why this stressful situation brings out the "Braveheart Warrior" in me, but it does. I get VERY defensive, and I just want to kick someone's butt.

Our awareness of our own stressors is a step in the right direction. Our goal, ultimately, is to minimize the power of our Lizard brain so it doesn't do a number on us when we are making decisions. Stressful situations happen on a continuum, and there are times when we simply don't see that we are in a state of stress and our Lizard brain is driving the bus.

Why then, do you want to make peace with your Lizard brain in the journey to find your Plan Be? Change is stressful. Working through the process to chart your path to being who you were put here to be means that you will have to let go of some of the bad habits that have kept you from pursuing your dreams. Over time, our Lizard brain becomes like an old friend to us, and when it is really good it becomes our voice. This is a dangerous place to live.

Reflect back on your three words for a moment, and you might see some Lizard brain thinking pop up.

Telling the world "I am these three things! This is what I have to offer. I want to be more of these three things!" can be stressful because you are naming and claiming something in your life, and by doing that you are taking a chance. Your Lizard brain might say this:

"Girl, you are too unique to be defined. Don't let someone back you in to a corner by choosing three words."

"You will probably choose the wrong words. You never were good at things like this anyway. Just pick three words and move on."

"There is nothing really special about you, so doing this activity is just going to reveal how very pathetic you are."

"Just because you pick those three words doesn't mean anything is going to change. You will just keep on doing the same ol' same ol' and never achieve anything."

"You are too old for this. You missed your chance to go after your dream. Give it up."

When I think about my three words: educate | liberate | entertain my Lizard brain wants to pipe in. She says to me:

"Educate? You. You didn't even finish your Ph.D. Why would anyone listen to you? You have never worked in Corporate America for goodness sakes. Who do you think you are? Too big for your britches I think."

"Entertainer? Are you Ellen? Look, you may be able to tell a few stories and get a few laughs, but you will never be a true entertainer. Give it up."

Don't you just want to punch my Lizard brain? Me too. She's a real pain.

Whether you are in a highly reactive stressful state or a mildly stressful state, your Lizard brain is never going to fail you. She will come out and she will go to work doing her thing. If you wanted to dig really, really deep, you would find that a lot of our Lizard brain conversations are deeply connected to past hurts, failures, and pains. Do these sound familiar:

"You are a fraud."

"You are fat and no one thinks you're pretty."

"You are stupid."

"It's OK that you are the way you are because you have had a hard life and it isn't your fault that _____."

"No one cares."

"People like you don't get to _____."

Over time, these highly critical response mechanisms lead us to create bad habits that sabotage our efforts to be successful. I see it all the time. Take the classic example that I run in to with professionals: Bob says: "I am just terrible at public speaking." This Lizard brain response is a reaction to feeling fear about public speaking. When confronted with the reality of having to do a presentation, Bob then engages in crazy practices like:

> Avoiding public speaking like it is a plague sent from God

> Firing off an impressive lists of the 117 reasons he can't be the guy who gives the presentation

> Ignoring the impact a great presentation could have on his career path

> Writing the presentation at the very last minute and winging it because planning and preparing make him feel stressed out

> Playing it super safe during the presentation

Your Lizard brain does not always attack, but can also present itself as your friend and helper. Take my friend "Alice." She is the mother of three and is 45 years old. Alice is college educated, smart, involved in the community, and has been a stay-at-home-mom for more than fifteen years. She recently revealed to me that she has a dream to become a nurse or do something in the health care industry where she can be a caregiver. I was really excited to learn this about her because it was something I did not know about her after years of friendship.

Naturally, I went into coaching mode and started asking her questions about this interest and how she would pursue this dream. It became clear after a few minutes that Alice was not going to do anything to make this dream a reality. Her powerful and sneaky Lizard brain had convinced her that her family could not function without her around to tend to their every need. Sound familiar?

She had created a story around her life that sounded like this: "I am a great mom and I do so much for my family. They really really need me 24-7 and I should be there for them." Her Lizard brain did not attack and hit below the belt but instead told her how wonderful and amazing she was as a mom and why would she ever give that role up?

All of us can insert our own "thing" that we get hung up on in the same way that Bob is hung up on public speaking or Alice who would not pursue a dream because she had created a powerful story of how wonderful and amazing she is in her current life.

For Brenda it's, "I don't do conflict."

For Sam it's, "I deserve a raise but they should know it. Why should I have to tell them?"

For Michelle it's, "I really want to go back to school, but who would do that at my age?"

And the list goes on and on. Every one of us has that thing that we avoid, dismiss, make excuses around why it isn't important, and I can guarantee you it is holding you back.

I will never get rid of my Lizard brain, and any efforts to do that are in vain. My Lizard brain is a part of me, but I have the power to minimize the impact she has on me. Later, when you are ready to claim your Plan Be you will likely feel energized, powerful, and ready to take on the world. What will you do the next day, the next week, and in the months to come when life happens, and you are tempted to resort to those bad habits that are spoken through your Lizard brain?

Let's revisit my presentation I opened up with earlier. As I sat there waiting for the president to finish her remarks, I went into my own head, and said this:

"I hear you Liizard brain. I know what you are doing, and I know you don't have my best interests at heart."

That shut her up.

Next, I chose to repeat the following over and over again instead of being in conversation with my Lizard brain.

I have something important to say.
I am here today because I was asked to be here.
What I say is going to have a positive impact on these
teachers, and they will be better
for having heard my presentation.

I said this inside my own mind over and over and over again until it was time to take the stage. This "mantra" of sorts was effective at calming my nerves. With each incantation, my heart rate slowed, my blood pressure equalized, I stopped shaking, and most importantly I combatted the "head noise" that was going on before hand.

Today, when I am stressed, I modify this mantra to suit the occasion. and it never fails to keep my Lizard brain at bay.

You have taken the time to identify your stressors and what HAPPENS to you when you are in a state of fight or flight. What will you do now, when a stressful situation presents itself? Planning out your response to stressful situations is one of the key steps in making peace with your Lizard brain and minimizing it's nasty effects. Draw inspiration from my "mantra" above that I use when I am stressed, and think of your own responses to stress. Here are a few ideas to get you started.

1. Breathe. Yes breathe. If you revisit the list of physiological and biochemical responses that happen when stressed, you will appreciate the power of simply breathing. Take a moment and take FIVE deep breaths. Breathe in through your nose and out through your mouth. With each breath count to five as you inhale and count to five as you exhale. Deep breathing allows you to slow down the powerful effects of your stress response and restore your clear and rational thinking.

2. Prepare a response. What will you say to your Lizard brain? Start with, "Hello Lizard brain. I had a feeling you would show up today." This funny and relaxed response is far more effective than, "Listen here you no good *&&^%$#. I don't know who you think you are…" You don't want to push back. Instead play nice, and don't let your Lizard brain "draw you off sides" as my husband says.

3. Next, replace your typical Lizard brain conversation with a mantra that reinforces what you are working toward. Structure your mantra in the affirmative. For example, don't say, "I am not a fraud," and instead say, "I care passionately about this topic and have taken a lot of time to master the content. I have stories and facts and figures and all kinds of great information to share that people will love!"

If you grew up in the 1980s on Saturday Night Live, then I am sure you have fond memories of the character Stuart Smalley. Stuart was a funny character who tapped into the growing market of self-help books, programs, and self-help gurus that were becoming more and more popular at that time. I remember him sitting with his hand mirror and repeating "I good enough, I am smart enough, and dog-gone-it people like me!"

I think people resist the idea of a mantra because of Stuart Smalley or other highly ridiculous examples of gurus who are all touchy and feely in their approach. I am not going to ask you to look into the mirror and repeat these mantras but I will tell you this: They can work. Just for the simple sake of minimizing the loudness of your Lizard brain, I encourage you to try this out and see for yourself.

You have found your three words, made your No-No list, and made peace with your Lizard brain.

You are ready for for Activity #4: Be Your Own Dictionary.

Everybody is a genius
but if you judge a fish
on its ability to climb a tree, it will live
its whole life believing it is stupid.
Albert Einstein

ACTIVITY #4:
Be Your Own Dictionary

When I was still teaching and listening to student speeches on the legalization of pot, illegal immigration, why the university should build a parking garage, and the other typical and tired college student speech topics, I would cringe when a student began a presentation with, "According to Webster's dictionary...."

It is perhaps the lamest, laziest, and most trite way to start a presentation and always reminded me of a a paper I wrote in English as a senior in high school that began with the old reliable, "According to Webster's dictionary..."

Today, the Webster's dictionary intro has been replaced with, "According to Wikipedia..." I have been out of the classroom for a good number of years now, but the last few semesters I was teaching, I outlawed Wikipedia as a source for a presentation!

The next activity in finding your Plan Be asks you to be your own dictionary. Forget Webster. You are going to define a few terms for yourself.

I was a high school debater. What I am trying to say is, in high school, I was very cool. I spent weekends with my debate partner arguing over issues like social security and retirement; prison overcrowding, and space exploration--the three topics (resolutions) for CX (cross examination) debate in 1989, 1990, and 1991. If you have not had the pleasure of seeing firsthand a high school CX debate round, you should. Find a local tournament that happens at a high school near you and drop in and see these kids in action. You will be inspired. High School debate kids are some of the smartest, most interesting, and most well-read kids you will ever meet. I am proud to belong to this elite club of nerds.

I digress...

When a CX debate round begins, the first thing you have to do is define your terms. This makes sense because how will you have a debate unless you agree with the other person on what you are debating in the first place. What, after all, is the definition of prison overcrowding I ask you? This is a term open to multiple interpretations. There have been CX debate rounds where the decision of who wins and who loses comes down to this very issue of how to define the terms.

In that same spirit, I ask you this: How should we define the word SUCCESS? What does it look like, act like, talk like, and walk like?

When I was in high school, almost every adult around me asked if I was going to law school. In their minds they equated my success as a high school debater with growing up to become an attorney. I got this so often, that my senior year of high school I had come to regard my future success plan as one routed through law school. I signed up for Mock Trial my senior year, excited for a taste of the courtroom.

If you are not familiar with mock trial, it is an excellent high school program where students play the role of attorney and witnesses around a pre-determined court case. The team prepares both sides of the trial, and then they compete against other schools. Our team that year was all female! I was an attorney, and my co-counsel was my best friend and debate partner, Amy Magness. The rest of our team played the roles of witnesses in the case.

We competed against the other high schools in our town and won the district tournament, giving us a spot at the state tournament in Dallas, Texas. We traveled to Dallas and competed but did not make it into the out rounds where we could win a first, second, third, or fourth place trophy. If I recall correctly, our team was disappointed to not go back home with a trophy.

I, on the other hand, could not have been happier. I hated mock trial. I found it boring, cumbersome, uninspired, and the take away for me was simple: If this is what it is like to be an attorney, then count me out, thank you very much. I thought being an attorney was going to look like an episode of L.A. Law. I would wear fabulous clothes, date a Jimmy Smits type character, and argue highly charged cases before a sour puss judge. Turns out, not so much.

I can't tell you how many times over the last twenty-something years I have paused and said to myself, "Thank you universe for the experience of mock trial." I am willing to bet many people have had the same kind of "a ha" moment where they learned that what they thought about something (being an attorney) turned out to be entirely different.

Why do I ask you to take the time to define success for yourself? I ask this of you because I believe that when we get to the heart of our success path, we will be happier, healthier, and more satisfied with our lives.

Defining my own success in terms that would resonate with me did not come till I was in my thirties. Oh the wisdom! As I started to build Bravo cc and think about the possibilities of what this adventure could become, I was mindful of one thing: I wanted to be there to get my girls when the school bell rang every day at 3:00. If I could have my own business, do what I love (teaching), and be there to pick up my girls when school let out--that would be my vision of success.

I didn't track the days from kindergarten to fifth grade, but I would be willing to bet that 90% of the time I was there to get my girls at the end of school. That felt good to me, and I know that while they may not appreciate it right now, they will one day.

Over the years, when my Lizard brain says things like:

"You could be making a lot more money if you would work harder to get more clients," or "There sure are a lot of people out there who are doing what you do, and they are getting famous! Why aren't you?" I have had to remind myself of my commitment to be accessible to my girls and pick them up when school let out at the end of the day.

Lately, with my 40th birthday on the horizon, my Lizard brain has been incredibly busy. She tells me, "You are turning 40. Most people at your age are far more successful than you are. You have missed the boat sister. You will never realize real professional success because you are almost dead."

"Shut up Lizard brain," I say, "I only have a few more years with my girls at home and I have many more years to enjoy professional success."

Naturally, any time you define a term for yourself there are going to be trade offs. My commitment to be accessible to my daughters for the full 18 years they are living in our home means that I don't seek out a great number of out-of-town gigs. If I travel once a month, that is just about right for me. It also means I don't do a lot of after-hours networking either. In business building, those after-hours events can be key to making new connections and finding new leads. I know that. But again, what is my definition of success?

For me, at this chapter in my life, success looks something like this:

1. Earn a steady income as a consultant who trains and educates my clients to be better communicators so they can stand out in the marketplace.
2. Maintain a 60/40 split between training projects and keynote speaking.
3. Be home to take my girls to school and pick them up when school gets out at least three or four days out of the week. Coordinate my schedule with my husband's, so he can be home to take and pick up when I can't.
4. Work from home as much as I can during the summer and have at least one "play day" during the week to go to the pool, go to Six Flags, go shopping, and just hang out with my kids.
5. Take two vacations a year with my husband and girls.
6. Take one vacation a year with my husband.
7. Have time to raise money for the What's Your Plan Be? Scholarship Fund.
8. Make time in my calendar to give back to the United Way of Denton County by offering a discounted rate to facilitate the Leader on Loan program.
9. Serve on the board of the Denton Public Schools Foundation.
10. Go to lunch with a girlfriend during the week if the occasion presents itself.

Over time, our idea of success changes and evolves (hopefully for the better). My youngest daughter, Trinity, is 11, and in seven years will graduate from high school and start the next chapter of her life. That is when I will be ready to implement the next phase of my success plan.

You see, I believe that if I am committed to the ten items above in my current success plan, I will be directly impacting what I am able to do in seven years when my girls have graduated and are in college. That is when I am going to take over the world! Not really, but I do know this-- In the year 2020 I will be forty-seven years old. My life will look like this:

1. I am an established trainer and speaker throughout the United States.
2. I will speak both nationally and internationally at conferences and conventions and be the keynote speaker.
3. I will have a best selling book that you can buy at Barnes and Noble (assuming they are still around....).
4. I will regularly be featured in magazines and TV shows to share my expertise as a communications consultant.
5. I will grow the What's Your Plan Be? scholarship fund to $25,000 a year in scholarships awarded to girls.
6. I will triple my income from 2013 to 2020 and position myself to be debt free.
7. I will work my #$% off for the next ten years, working on my business in a way that I have never done before because I now have the time, wisdom, and experience.
8. I will contribute monetarily to manifesting our dream to spend our 60s traveling the globe, living abroad, and having adventures.
9. I will be healthy and happy and free of baggage.
10. I will be 100% comfortable in my own skin and go after the things I want to do without fear of what anyone will think of me.

When I lay in bed at night, I envision myself doing these things. I have seen myself on Oprah's couch talking about What's Your Plan Be? I see myself in magazines answering women's questions about how to take back their lives and own their own success story. I see myself on the stage in front of thousands of people who want to hear me speak. And I look good. I look really good. I have on some sassy shoes, a great looking dress, my hair is silver and gorgeous, ("Why no I don't color my hair. This is just the way it looks!"), and there is a twinkle in my eye. You might think I am crazy to go so far as to fantasize about this life I have planned, but I think when we stop dreaming, we die a little inside.

I will never stop dreaming.

I don't want you to stop dreaming either.

How then will you define success? Think about what success looks like right now for you. Challenge yourself to name FIVE things that you want to start doing right now to move toward your success plan.

I will _____

I want to _____

I can _____

I believe _____

I know _____

This activity is something you can do daily, weekly, monthly, and of course annually. Today, as I am typing this, it is Monday. Monday is typically not a fun-day for me. Here is how I tackled my success list for today.

I will: write for two hours and edit for one hour.

I want to: walk the dog, fold laundry, watch Mad Men.

I can: take the time to respond to emails and send my handout to Tanya Ramer for Thursday's workshop in Waco even though I don't think those things are fun. It will take me less than an hour.

I believe: this is going to be a great day, and I will get a lot done.

I know: I tend to get wrapped up in things and can ignore what is going on around me. I will set timers to make sure I stay on task.

This is an effective activity for me because it keeps me on task. I will be honest with you. When I woke up this morning, the first thing I thought was, "Can I take a nap today?" You see, I stayed up with my husband last night till 12:45am watching the Survivor finale. Not smart. But I did it, and this morning I was paying the price.

Success...
Define your success plan
daily, weekly,
monthly, annually.
Then ask, where do I want to
be in five years, ten years,
twenty years.

I know that taking a nap on a Monday is a pretty stupid idea and won't make for a great start to my week. Over coffee, I laid out my success plan for Monday and then got to work knowing that if I charted my success plan for the next eight hours, I would resist the urge to nap. I started with the not-so-fun task of answering emails and putting together a hand out for Thursday's workshop I am teaching. As usual, it is never as bad as I think it is going to be, and in less than an hour I was done with these tasks and ready to move on to writing.

Success is not the only word that you should stop and take the time to define. Other words can get the same treatment. For example, how do you define: Family, Parenting, Friendship, Weekend, Down-Time, Vacation, Hobby, Love, Commitment, Discipline, Happiness, Peace, Sacrifice, Contentment, Boss, Team Player, and Home? All these loaded words can mean many different things to different people. Other people's definitions can get in the way of our own definition, and if we are not careful, we can look up to find that we are living out someone else's definition.

By taking the time to define these words for yourself and share them with those around you, you are taking control of your success plan.

Before you move on to the next activity. Define the following words for yourself. Feel free to add you own words to the list as well.

DEFINE SUCCESS:

DEFINE FAMILY:

DEFINE CAREER:

DEFINE WEEKEND:

DEFINE FRIENDSHIP:

DEFINE PARENTING:

DEFINE SMART:

I am a BIG fan of TED. You will meet TED later when you learn to be a Presentation Super Hero. In the meantime, I want to introduce you to just one presentation from TED by Mike Rowe, famous for his wonderful show *Dirty Jobs*. (Go here to watch Rowe's excellent presentation http://www.ted.com/talks/mike_rowe_celebrates_dirty_jobs.html or search Mike Rowe in the search bar at www.ted.com)

I watched this presentation for the first time about a month ago, and I was struck by the message that the happiest people he has met are those who work in jobs that most people would assume are a miserable way to earn one's living. From plumbers to pig farmers, and every conceivable dirty job in between, Rowe challenges his audience to re-asses the value of "hard work and happiness."

Rowe's presentation struck a chord for me because it reminded me of my own father. Not "smart" by traditional standards (college degree, well-read, high grades in school), my dad is one of the most hard-working and smartest men I have ever known. He may have never negotiated million dollar deals, but give my dad a piece of wood and he can make just about anything you ask for. Give him a broken anything, and I bet he could fix it. Give him a patch of dirt and I know he could grow something on it. My dad is smart. I didn't fully appreciate this until I was an adult and I understood that smart comes in so many different flavors. What an incredible gift that is to realize that my definition of smart should be expanded to include all varieties of smart-ness.

Albert Einstein, easily the smartest man of his century, and perhaps in the whole of history put it best: "Everybody is a genius. But if you judge a fish on its ability to climb a tree, it will live its whole life believing it is stupid." If Einstein understood this it only makes sense that we too embrace the idea that how we DEFINE words like smart, and genius, and intelligence matters.

You are taking back your own power to define the words that matter to you. Put them somewhere you will see them as a reminder to yourself of how you see the world. Be prepared to use these definitions when your Lizard brain goes into overdrive and starts telling you lies about your own life.

Now you are ready to get to the next step: Let's break a few rules, shall we?

Civilization had too
many rules for me,
so I did my best to rewrite them.
Bill Cosby

Activity #5:
Break Rules

"What is the key to success?"

This is a question I get asked all the time and my answer is this:

C O U R A G E

A high IQ is great, passion is good too. Being organized, a people person, and dressing "like a boss" are all good. But....none of those things are necessary ingredients for success.

Courage is.

You cannot be successful without having the courage to put yourself out there, take a chance, and see what happens.

When I think of courage I am reminded of a few amazing people I've been fortunate to cross paths with::

"Chase", a college student in my classroom who was twenty-five years old and had suffered multiple strokes after overdosing on some pretty hard core drugs. He had limited use of his left side, and he spoke with a pronounced speech impediment. I can imagine a required college class in speech communication was the last thing he wanted to do. But he did it. Chase completed all four required speeches and he never lost his sense of humor. He was the most courageous student I have ever had in my classroom.

"Richard", a deaf employee with one of my clients, who signed up to take my FRONT AND CENTER workshop. This workshop is all about public speaking, and I will not lie, I was a little taken aback when I entered the room that morning and met Richard and his interpreter. At the end of the workshop, every participant gets up and gives a five minute presentation. Richard took his turn and working with his interpreter gave a fantastic presentation. I have never forgotten that day and Richard's courage to take a risk and learn how to be a stand out public speaker, despite his inability to speak and he taught me a thing or two about life.

Let me grab a Kleenex really quick.

OK. I am back.

In our professional lives, the truly courageous are those who are willing to break a few rules to reach their goals. Now, I am not talking about breaking the LAW. I am more interested in breaking rules that reside around the old "this is how we have always done things" mindset (Plan A).

I want you to Be a Rule Breaker.

I have never done illegal drugs in my life, and while I can reference some times in my life when I overdosed on chocolate, it didn't get me high. My high in life comes when I get in front of an audience and create an experience with them where learning happens, lightbulb moments materialize, and we laugh, tell stories, and connect with one another.

I could not experience this "high" if I were not willing to break a few rules about what a presentation experience should look like. I will detail bad presentations in the next chapter, but for now let me give you one solid example.

The RULE:
Create Power Point slides that are littered with fifteen bullet points. Let the slides be the presentation and the presenter stands there and reads the slides to the audience.

I am a RULE BREAKER:
I am certain that my commitment to creating a slide experience that you do not find anywhere else is one of the keys to my success. I regularly have audience participants ask me if
a.) I pay someone to create my slides (hmmm maybe they doubt my creativity?)
b.) Would I be willing to share my slides with them?
c.) What do I charge to create slides for a client?

The journey to find your Plan Be requires you to walk out on that high dive, look down into the deep, deep water, close your eyes, and jump. You will be scared, you will be uncomfortable, and you may swan dive or belly flop, but at least you did something! You lived. You tried it. You won't have to lay on your death bed and wonder, "What if..."

If I have not fully inspired you to consider the life of a rule breaker, perhaps the well-regarded T.S. Eliot can. He writes, "Only those who will risk going too far can possibly find out how far one can go."

If that did not do the trick, let me encourage you to take a five minute break. Go to your Pinterest account (you have a Pinterest account right? You have to have a Pinterest account!) and click on the Quotes tab. Spend a few minutes reading through the quotes posted there. I would venture to say that 75% of them are inspirational and motivational in nature and will "fill your cup." When your cup is overflowing, come back to the book and pick up where you left off.

*Before bed each night, I open the quotes tab on my Pinterest app on my phone and spend a few minutes reading through the many quotes that are posted on there and taking a few minutes at the end of my day to be in a state of true gratitude and counting my blessings.

> **"You can either fit in or stand out. Not both."**
> **Seth Godin in**
> *Linchpin*

Those who regularly fill their cup with inspiration and motivation are far more likely to be ready to break a few rules.

"OK Libby, I am ready. Let's break a few rules. Can you kindly tell me what rules I should be breaking?"

"Yes. Yes I can," says me.

In some ways, you have probably already been thinking about this idea. When I presented the concept of Plan A | Plan B | Plan Be, I laid the ground work for breaking rules. Please understand the concept of breaking rules is rather simple. It looks like this:

Plan A is where the rules live. They are couched in phrases like

"This is how we have always done things"

"Well our family are all attorneys so what do you mean you want to be a fashion designer"

"You should study something that is safe and reliable like business management"

"That is not how a young lady should behave"

"Boys love sports. Is something wrong with you?"

and on and on and on.

Plan B is living life in reaction mode. The rules of Plan A don't always work out and people must resort to a back-up plan. At the heart of this thinking lies this truth, "Plan A is right and I will follow it. Oops Plan A didn't work, what's our back-up plan?" and 9 times out of 10, people go right back to their Plan A thinking.

You see instances of this thinking all the time. I am sure the following will be familiar to you:

Plan A says	Plan BE Says
Employee Handbooks make sense.	Get rid of the handbook and keep it simple. Think Google's mission statement: "Do no Evil!"
If you have a problem with someone refer it on to HR for them to handle.	Have a conversation with people, be honest and direct.
Only the people at the top of the food chain have good ideas.	People at all levels of the organization have valuable ideas and should contribute them.
Go on an interview and cross my fingers they call me and offer the job.	Call two days later, and ask if they have made a decision. Say "I want this job. Am I your first choice for the job?"
Preparing a 57 slide deck for your next presentation riddled with bullet points and clip art.	Ditching the Power Point and finding your inner Tina Turner. You are the Presentation!
Staying in a job you hate because you need the paycheck.	Taking a chance and going back to school to finish your degree to get the job you have always wanted!
Ordering a template business card from Vista Print (it's free!).	Hiring a REAL designer to create you a kick $%^& business card that looks like NO ONE else's!
Crossing your fingers and hoping you get what you want.	ASKING for what you want!
Working 80 hours a week.	Working smarter and getting the same amount of work done (maybe even more!) in 40 hours.
Not taking your 2 weeks of vacation to show how much you care about your job.	Taking vacation and re-booting and re-connecting to YOU. Read books, take a nap, watch those movies you have been wanting to see and come back to work refreshed and reinvigorated!

Plan Be is for Rule Breakers! Plan Be says "I want to live MY plan, and that may not look like your plan or your plan or his plan or her plan. It is MY plan. I wrote my own set of rules!" Rule breakers do not apologize, justify, diminish, or circle around their plan. They do it.

Rule Breakers:

Name It.
Claim It.
Live It.

In the spirit of the greatest rule breakers around, let me give you the starting point to begin breaking rules.

One of the first places you can be a rule breaker is to break someone's expectations for you. People have expectations of you, your business, and your industry. Let's take a tax accountant as our example. We expect a tax accountant to be all about the numbers; cold and calculating. We expect him or her to be un-personable, analytical, and well, boring. Do you fit this formula or do you break the rules or expectations in some way? Don't get your feelings hurt over the assessment of your industry. These are stereotypes, and we ALL bring them to the table whenever we interact with someone. Your job is to make us question those stereotypes. What is your first thought when I say Salesman?

Huh? Right? Sales is a dirty word for a lot of people. We think unethical, slimy, car salesman, underhanded, and out for their own interests. Is this true for all salespeople? No. I know some amazing sales people. I am married to one. My point is simple--you are going to be measured by the expectations/experiences/stereotypes/prejudices people bring to the exchange just as you will bring your own stereotypes to them too.

1. What EXPECTATIONS do people have about you?

2. What STEREOTYPES do people have about your profession?

3. What STEREOTYPES do people have about your industry?

4. What STEREOTYPES do people have about your organization?

5. Now for the good stuff. What EXPECTATION or STEREOTYPE are you defying to stand out in the marketplace (for all the right reasons)?

Back to our tax accountant. Just having a personality and sharing it with your clients will help to break the pattern--it will make you remarkable.

Your clients will tell their friends, "Our tax accountant Mike is a really cool guy. Man, when we first met with him, he had this big Buddha statue on his desk, he was listening to Red Hot Chili Peppers, and he was wearing Toms! Can you imagine? But he is great. I could really talk to this guy."

Breaking the rules sounds great, but it also is a little risky. It makes us feel uncomfortable and uneasy. We get so used to doing business as usual that when someone comes along and says, "Let's try it a different way," we get a big lump in our throat. When should you break the rules? If you are getting the results you hope for every time, then you are probably doing something right. But if you feel stagnant or like you are quickly losing ground, it is time to shake things up.

Many businesses and professionals feel like that right now as our economy lags. Competition is fierce in a way that it has never been as companies who never went after your share of the market are now competing for the same clients you have worked with for years. Professionals are finding it daunting to be in the job market competing against other well-qualified applicants for the same job.

Under these conditions:

NOW IS THE TIME TO START BREAKING THE RULES.

When you break the rules, the payoff can be amazing. Let me give you a few examples.

A few years ago one of my clients had a presentation to prepare. The project was an outdoor learning center for a school district in the Houston area. We had done in-depth presentation training, and they took what they learned and applied it to the presentation. Unfortunately, not everyone was on board with their approach. In fact, one of the decision makers in this firm (who works at a different office), called and told me, "They have lost their minds! What were they thinking?"

After I calmed him down and got the details, it turned out that this group prepared a presentation that looked NOTHING like presentations their firm had always done. They had broken the rules. As luck would have it, I was headed to Houston that week to work, and said I would stop by and have them do the presentation for me.

The decision makers for who would land the contract for this outdoor learning center were comprised of various school district employees, including the superintendent, school principals, school board members, teachers, and curriculum designers.

Within minutes of starting their presentation for me, I couldn't wipe the smile from my face. I felt like a proud mama as I watched their clever, smart, and 100% audience-centered presentation.

How did they break the rules?

Rule: Prepare a presentation that you would like.

Rule Breaker: Prepare a presentation that your audience will like and respond to.

Most professionals miss the mark with their presentations because they don't build the presentation for their client--they build it for themselves. Without even realizing it, they create a presentation that they would love to sit in the audience and listen to. But how many architects do you know who design projects for other architects? They don't.

In this case, this group's audience was educators. Knowing that, they built their presentation around the wants, needs, and desires of educators. Because this was an outdoor learning center, they removed their "corporate nod" photos from the PowerPoint to introduce the team and replaced them with pictures of each person outdoors with their family in nature. These were pictures that already existed. They didn't stage the pictures and pretend to love the outdoors. This one "breaking the rules" move on their part was brilliant. It told the decision making group, "Not only are we architects, but we're people who love the outdoors, have school aged children, and you can connect to us."

An added touch to the presentation was a soundtrack that played during the presentation--a soundtrack of outdoor nature noises like the wind rustling through the trees, birds chirping, and insects buzzing. To an architect this sounds ludicrous. To an educator it sounds like music.

Their presentation hit the mark, and just a few days later, they learned their team had been selected for the project. The takeaway is simple: If what you are doing isn't working then try something different for goodness sakes. Shake things up!

1. Get new people involved to bring their ideas to the table.
2. Look outside your industry to learn best practices from other industries and see if it might get some mileage for you.
3. But do something! Don't keep doing the same old tired, business as usual approach, and hope for new results. That is the definition of insanity!

If you are still a little leery about the idea of being a rule breaker, know this: People who are rule breakers are more successful.

I listen to 106.1 KISS FM every morning when I am in the car taking my girls to school. One morning, the DJ's talked about Robert Suchan, a 6 foot 5 inch guy living in Long Island, who earns $250,000 a year selling Tupperware. How does he do it? Unlike his colleagues who sell Tupperware, he has found a character named "Aunt Barbara" living inside of him, and she wants to sell some Tupperware!

I was instantly intrigued by his story and came home and Googled "Man sells Tupperware dressed as woman" (God bless you Google!), and found what I was looking for. In an interview with a local news station, he explained the appeal. "Tupperware kind of had a reputation that people really didn't want to go to the parties," Suchan said, according to WCBS-TV. "They thought they were boring; they were going to be conned into buying things, and I thought, you know, if she just turned it into a little bit of a show, and she had another reason for people to come, the Tupperware would just sell itself." That was the birthplace of Aunt Barbara, a sassy, fast-talking woman who does more than sell Tupperware. She entertains at home parties and has made a Tupperware Party Invitation the hottest ticket in town!

I don't know a lot of Tupperware sales people, but I will bet you an R.C. Cola and a Moon Pie that 90% of them do not make $250,000 a year selling Tupperware. In fact, I will go double or nothing and bet you that they don't even make $100,000 a year. Suchan's success is simple: He broke rules. The first rule? Men don't sell Tupperware. The second rule? Selling Tupperware can be an event, an experience, a night out at a comedy club type experience. He took a risk, provided an experience that women can't get anywhere else, and the proof is in the pudding (which he probably puts in a nice piece of Tuppeware and into the fridge).

To be remarkable and get people talking about you, you have to do something that everyone else around you is not doing, and that means breaking a rule or two. That is the name of the game in today's marketplace, and while it probably does not mean you have to wear drag and invent a sassy character, the reality is that you must do something- anything - to stand out. For many people the opportunity to be a rule breaker passes them by because they are so deeply entrenched in the "business as usual" model.

For those people, inspiration is in order. I present to you: Southwest Airlines. How, you ask, is Southwest Airlines a rule breaker in their industry? Consider these things:

1. Since 1973 Southwest Airlines has been profitable.
2. They have NEVER had layoffs.

RULE BREAKER:

Employees first
Customers second
Shareholders third

3. Herb Kellerher's formula for success is simple: employees first, customers second, shareholders third.

4. Everyone at the top of the food chain is not too good to do any job that needs to be done.

5. They have stayed 100% committed to their core value: "We are the low fare airline" and all their decisions have been funneled through this value.

To understand their rule breaker mentality, look at former Southwest Airlines President, Colleen Barrett's, attitude on common industry standards (Plan A's) on how work gets done versus how she sees things.

On work-life balance:
"I don't understand why an employee should have one personality at work and another outside of work. We do offer you the ability and encourage you to come into the business world as who you are. We hire you for your individuality, and we aren't going to try to spend six months molding you into our corporate culture."

On Southwest's hiring policy:
"We tend to hire for attitude and train for skills—but don't get nervous, we don't hire pilots who can't fly a plane."

On "The customer is always right":
"We make no bones about telling a customer when they are wrong. We will not tolerate bad treatment of our people."

Just these three things alone indicate that this is a rule breaking organization. Her philosophy of how to run a business flies in the face of decades of Plan A business philosophy. These rule breaker practices pay off. Consider their leadership.

In today's Plan A organizational culture, respect and awe for leaders can be hard to find. This is not the case at Southwest Airlines. Herb Kelleher, former president and CEO, is so admired both inside and outside his organization that upon his retirement in 2007, the Southwest Airlines Pilots Association took out a full page ad in *USA Today* to thank him for his hard work and dedication.

The ad read "As you step down from the SWA Board of Directors, the pilots of Southwest Airlines would like to thank you, Herb, for 38 years of positively outrageous service to our Company and our pilots. It has been an honor and a privilege."

Are you kidding me? What did you do when your boss retired? You probably pitched in with everyone else to get him/her an ice cream cake right? Can you tell me any other time that the leader of an organization was given this level of thank you? I have yet to come across anything like it. These pilots paid $150,000 for their full page, four color ad in *USA Today*. That's a lot of love right there.

To fully illustrate my point let's look at another remarkable airline company: American Airlines.

From a purely anecdotal perspective I can testify that the culture of AA is far different from that of Southwest Airlines. I fly ten to twelve times a year on AA, and my husband also flies AA on a regular basis. We live in an AA hub and that often means AA is the "best choice" because of convenience and pricing. Despite these two driving factors, my bad experiences with AA outnumber the good ones. If I were to choose one word to describe AA it would be this: Demoralized. Now don't get me wrong. Not every person I have dealt with at AA has been Debbie Downer. But many of them are. It isn't hard to imagine why.

Couple that with our former neighbor who is a flight attendant for AA. On the back of his car are a variety of stickers that collectively is a big middle finger to the powers that be at AA. In fact, on occasion, these stickers were apparently not enough, and he would get shoe polish and write on his car windows "I work for crooks," and "AA steals from their employees." Ouch.

Take all that and consider another full page ad taken out in *USA Today* by The Allied Pilots Association in 2008 (representing American Airline's 12,000 pilots).

They wrote:

> We're embarrassed that so many passengers are inconvenienced and dissatisfied and hope you'll accept our apologies for our airline's unreliability. Why is American Airlines failing its customers? Due to mismanagement, our airline doesn't have enough workers to run dependably. It also doesn't keep enough spare parts to ensure prompt repairs — and with the industry's second-oldest fleet, the need for repairs is more and more frequent. American Airlines needs to reinvest in our airline, and do so quickly.

Yowza.

I believe that the fundamental difference between these two organizations who provide the same service is the difference between Plan A thinking and Plan BE thinking. The core values of Southwest Airlines are remarkably different from every other airline they compete with. They are mavericks and rule breakers.

But does this difference impact the success of these two organizations? Yes and there is plenty of evidence to support my position. Consider, for example, statistics for 2010 from the Department of Transportation. Out of nine major carriers, Southwest Airlines and American Airlines are measured along five categories and ranked as follows:

On Time Arrival:
Southwest Airlines ranks 6th and American Airlines is 7th

Canceled Flights:
Southwest Airlines is 2nd with American Airlines coming in 7th

Baggage handling:
Southwest Airlines is 6th with American Airlines coming in 9th

Not Bumping Passengers:
Southwest ranks 7th and American comes in 4th

Customer complaints:
Southwest comes in at 4.4 while American comes in at 6.4

You can do your own research study and see if it bears out. Ask people for their opinion of the two airlines and measure the reactions you receive. I am willing to bet good money that Southwest has a far better reputation than AA.

I hope the illustration of these two organizations in the same industry make my point about the importance of being a rule breaker.

It is easy to see that Southwest Airlines is a rule breaking company. They are one of the usual suspects along with Apple, Nike, and Starbucks that are the leaders in their industry because they are willing to do something different that no one else is doing. They write their own rules.

But how can YOU be a rule breaker? That is the burning question. It is one thing to understand on a cerebral level that breaking rules is good but the act is a much different animal. First, you must legitimately be breaking the rule versus posing. Manufactured rule breakers are easy to sniff out. They hire an image consultant and create a campaign to tell a story that LOOKS like they are mavericks when in fact they are not. I am reminded of many of the failed attempts by Microsoft over the last two years to present themselves as hip, cool, and cutting edge when in fact, that is not who they are.

This kind of lie is much like the interview process when an employer and potential new hire make a lot of grand statements about who they are ("At Acme Brick we are a family company. We put our people first!" and "On average I have saved my clients one million dollars"). It doesn't take long to sniff out the untruths because our experience will be the measuring stick we use to decide if this person or organization is in fact a real rule breaker. And so many times we are disappointed.

A second risk is that you SAY you are breaking a rule that everyone else says they are breaking too.

Architects love to talk about how innovative they are. As an outsider to this industry, I have had the pleasure of working with a number of firms and assessing their competition, and guess what? Every architecture firm SAYS they are innovative, but when I line everyone up, I have a really tough time seeing just how it is that they are innovative. It is one thing to SAY you are innovative, it is a far different thing to actually Be innovative.

You are not going to be a poser. You are not going to say you are breaking a rule that everyone else is breaking too! You are going to be the real deal. What follows then are a few ideas to get you started in your new life as a rule breaker.

RULE: *Titles natter*
RULE BREAKER: *Titles are stupid. Use Your Three Words in place of titles.*

No one really cares (except your mom) that you are the president, CEO, or director of XYZ. People don't connect to titles, they connect to people. On your next order of business cards, replace your title with your three words and see what happens!

RULE: *Tell them everything you know*
RULE BREAKER: *Edit. Yes. Edit.*

I know that that act of editing may not seem like a "living on the edge" activity for your new rule breaker lifestyle, but hear me now, believe me later: The ability to edit your message to the very core of what you have to offer is a rule breaking act! Most people, brands, and organizations throw up on every thing they have their name on with CONTENT, CONTENT, CONTENT, and it is overwhelming. If you can learn to keep your message simple without telling me everything you have ever known since the beginning of ever, you will stand out from all the noise out there. I PROMISE you!

RULE: *Be all things to all people*
RULE BREAKER: *SPECIALIZE*

You cannot be an expert at everything. In today's marketplace, the ability to name and claim a specific area of expertise and OWN it is what will separate you from the masses. Choosing your three words + building your No-No list is a step in the right direction. You are already getting closer to "that thing you do" that no one else can do as well as you. If you need the language to think through this idea simply fill in the blank:

I specialize in _____.

My speciality is _____.

There is no one out there who can _____ like I can.

RULE: *Look out for number one*
RULE BREAKER: *Give first*

The act of giving first, and then receiving, is a strategy that can separate you from the masses and help you go share your spiritual gifts with others in ways that are meaningful. It has been my own experience that when I share my gifts with others with an open heart, good things follow. Take the example of someone who is in the job market looking for employment in a down economy. The focus is all on ME! ME! ME! trying to find a job. But what if...instead of focusing on finding the job, you gave away your talents and strengths? Let's say, for example, you spend 30 hours a week job seeking. Why not take 10 to 15 of those hours and volunteer your time and energy for a worthy cause? Yes, you are not getting paid. But...you might just meet the person who offers you your next job while you are volunteering.

RULE: *Sell your soul to your career/job*
RULE BREAKER: *Set boundaries*

I remember hearing about the term "mid-life crisis" a lot as a kid, and in my own mind thought: "Man turning 40 sure is going to suck because that's when people have their mid-life crisis." But now? Now you don't just have the mid-life crisis, you have the quarter-life crisis too. My land! People are experiencing melt downs in their twenties, thirties, forties, fifties, and sixties, and I am convinced much of it has to do with not setting clear boundaries in our lives. Plan A is a true believer in working 50+ hours a week. I am not. I know all the head talk you can engage in to convince yourself that working non stop, not taking care of yourself, and ignoring family and friends makes sense, but it doesn't.

This is not an exhaustive list but will point you in the right direction for becoming a rule breaker. The ball is in your court.

Last night my husband was laying in bed watching *Moneyball*. On Sony Pictures website, they describe this film as:

> Oakland A's general manager Billy Beane (Brad Pitt) challenges the system and defies conventional wisdom when he is forced to rebuild his small-market team on a limited budget. Despite opposition from the old guard, the media, fans, and their own field manager (Philip Seymour Hoffman), Beane - with the help of a young, number-crunching, Yale-educated economist (Jonah Hill) - develops a roster of misfits...and along the way, forever changes the way the game is played. (http://www.sonypictures.com/movies/moneyball/)

If you have not seen the movie, add it to your to-do list. I had already seen the movie before with my daughter Trinity, but I sat down with Mark and watched it for a few minutes. It occurred to me that they never make movies about the people who played it safe, followed all the rules, and lived a nice, neat, and boring (robot) life. The GREAT movies are about the people who stepped out and did something different. These people are surrounded by naysayers, much like Billy Beane was, and yet they move forward anyway because they are compelled by some force that tells them, "Yes, you can do this!"

Success is built on a solid foundation of courage. The people who are willing to break a few rules, and accept the consequences of those choices are the ones who find their way. They may not do a swan dive the first time, or even the first 100 times, but they know that with commitment and the courage to get back up that those belly flops will become a swan dive in due time!

You are on your way to capturing the real power of naming your Plan Be! Our next activity might make you hungry, so grab a snack and join me to answer the question, "What do you bring to the table?"

BLOG EXTRA!
I heart Seth Godin and the Corporate Types who just don't get IT!

I spent part of my time this morning going through my marked up copy of *"Linchpin,"* Seth Godin's newest book. I wish I could call him up and personally thank him for writing this book because he has articulated the very essence of what I do at Bravo cc and why we do it. **I make people indispensable**. What a relief to have a WORD that encapsulates what I DO.

I teach my clients to have a great elevator speech prepared and ready for anytime, anyplace, and anyone, but the truth is I have struggled coming up with the perfect explanation for what Bravo cc does. Sometimes I answer: "I do training and development workshops to help people sharpen their communication skills," but I know that this answer is lacking what I call "the big So WHAT?" So what, you improve communication skills? Big deal. Other times I have said, "I teach soft skills training" because this word SOFT SKILLS had some currency a few years back, and I figure if I speak the language of the average every day corporate-type person they will get it.

Sometimes I am cheeky and answer with, "I am a superhero fighting the forces of evil that result in bad presentations and bad communication skills," which is kind of fun but still lacks that certain something.

And then along comes Seth (yeah we are on a first name basis in my own mind),and he puts pen to paper (finger to keyboard more likely) and tells me what I am. I wish like heck I could MAKE everyone read *Linchpin*. I wish even more I could MAKE the people who cross my path, and don't get it read this book. But alas I cannot. What I can do though, is pull out some of the key things in *Linchpin* that help explain how I help make people indispensable. I have six pages of notes. I will just pull out a few here today to illustrate my point. Seth has summed up the premise of his book here:

The Only way to succeed is to be REMARKABLE, to be talked about.

Why this matters to me:

The work I do is all about helping people be REMARKABLE. I heard once that someone criticized what I do for their organization as irrelevant because I don't work in their industry. But the qualities that make someone or some organization remarkable go well beyond industry. REMARKABLE is not about the widget you make, but all the things that come along with the purchase of the widget.

So you can sell hubcaps, straws, windshield wipers, or copiers and the elements of what make your service remarkable will be shared across all these examples. Don't get me wrong--you must know your product, you must know your industry, but in the world of remarkable there comes a point where you and your competition reach a threshold on the quality of the product or service and what separates the good from the great are the things you deliver in addition to the product.

Seth writes "When your organization becomes more human, more remarkable, faster on it's feet, and more likely to connect directly with customers, it becomes indispensable. The very thing that made your employee a linchpin makes YOU a linchpin. An organization of indispensable people doing important work is remarkable, profitable, and indispensable in and of itself."

That is what I DO! I help people and organizations be MORE HUMAN. The truth is that there are so many layers of interaction that occur between the organization and the client that are added together to make up how people see you/the organization. Knowing this, I approach my client from the perspective that EVERYONE in the organization AT ALL LEVELS can stand to learn some new things, refine their communication skills, and come closer to knowing what their strengths/talents are that will make the organization more human.

I also help an organization identify the right people for the right kinds of interaction. Do you hate public speaking and avoid it all cost? OK. I will train you and give you the tools you need to do a competent job when you must get in front of an audience, but I also know well enough that if this is NOT your talent then why keep putting you in front of an audience?

What if instead I found the people in the organization who already have a natural talent for public speaking and plug them in to these activities? And it usually turns out that the person who is not so great at public speaking has other talents that are sorely needed in the equation like interacting one-on-one with the client. This process is where I start to help people become indispensable!

Through training and development and one-on-one coaching I am able to get the right people doing the right things in the organization to help produce the right outcomes.

The last thing I want to highlight in this post is Seth's great explanation of why people like me bring value to what you do.

He writes: "There are books and classes that can teach you how to do most of the things discussed in this book. And while many copies are sold and many classes attended, the failure rate is astonishingly high. It's not because the books and classes aren't good. It's because the RESISTANCE (your Lizard brain) is stronger.

When the resistance tells you not to listen to something, read something, or attend something--GO! DO IT! It's not an accident that successful people read more books."

All I can say is AMEN and PREACH ON! My goal is to work with people who are in a constant state of learning. People who ask a lot of questions, challenge the status quo and know that if they don't do these two things the world is going to pass them by. Successful organizations and people must be nimble and quick in today's rapidly changing environment where nothing is guaranteed anymore. Competition is fierce, and everyone wants their piece of the pie, and heck, they are happy to take your piece too. And people and organizations who are not paying attention often look up and find "holy Moses they took my piece of the pie!" Well yeah....

I like hanging out with people who get the Big So What. For me, the Big So What is this: Being indispensable comes down to relationships and your ability to successfully navigate your way through all the many layers of those relationships. At Bravo cc I help my clients do that.

And if you are one of those weird "always learning" kinda people then pick up Seth's book, *Linchpin*. The few hours it takes you to read it will be time well spent. Now, go be indispensable.

My hope still is to leave
the world a bit better than
when I got here
Jim Henson

Activity #6:
What Do You Bring to the Table?

Chicken and Dumplings
Cornbread
Fried Okra
Chocolate Pie
Homemade Vanilla Ice Cream
Cheese Rolls

Oh my!

Some of my fondest childhood memories involve time spent with extended family members on both my mom's and dad's sides of the family. Like many families, we had our own traditions that defined what it meant to be an Eddleman or a Carson. We love a good game of 42 (played with dominos), croquet, Spades (a card game), signing church songs using our own family copy of church hymnals, and of course we have a deeply religious relationship with food.

Everyone has their specialty dish or recipe that they bring to any gathering, and quite honestly, it would not be the same if each person did not "bring it to the table." My mom is expected to show up at any gathering with a chocolate pie and a coconut pie. She rarely stops there though, and adds a few more goodies like pecan pie, Toll House pie, cherry-cream pie, and her famous chocolate chip cookies.

My husband is the cook in our family, and when we gather with his family he is committed to preparing his famous pasta salad or avocado pico.

What do you bring to the table?

I have the great pleasure of working with a leadership program through the United Way called "Leaders on Loan." Organizations "loan" their leaders to the United Way for eight months, and these leaders complete a professional leadership development program + run a fundraising program called "Dine United." My piece of the program is teaching the leadership development workshops and challenging each leader to push themselves further into new territory to develop their leadership skills. In our first workshop, I ask the question: "What do you bring to the table?" In response, I typically receive back a lot of deer-in-the-headlights looks.

You are already on your way to answering this question with absolute confidence because the activities you have completed were leading you to this place. But why is it important that you be ready to answer this question anytime, anyplace, and with anyone?

The answer is simple really. I want you to answer this question now because it tells the world who you are, what you do, and why it matters. When you take the time to practice your answer to this question, you won't get caught off guard when you are asked this or a similar question.

Look back at your three words. Within your three words are the beginning to answering the question "What do you bring to the table?"

Before we address HOW to put together your answer, understand that there are multiple ways to ask the question.

 WHAT DO YOU BRING TO THE TABLE?

"Tell me a little bit about yourself...."
"Why should we hire you over Bob?"
"I like your product/service but, I am just not sure..."
"We are considering three companies for the contract, and yours is one of them..."
"I am not sure you are right for this job, project, team..."

When you are asked one of these questions, you will be ready to answer! Structure your answer around the following three things:
1. This is who you are.
2. This is what you do.
3. This is why it matters.

Below is my own example to get you thinking.

WHO YOU ARE:
"Hi I am Libby Spears with Bravo cc, a communications consulting adventure that provides practical solutions to communication conundrums."

WHAT YOU DO:
"I work with professionals to be game changers in their organization, industry, and the marketplace by taking their communication skills seriously. How? By addressing public speaking, storytelling and branding, and leadership and interpersonal skills through training and coaching programs that deliver results."

THIS IS WHY IT MATTERS:
"The marketplace is crowded and competitive. The name of the game is finding ways to stand out and connect to clients and customers in meaningful ways. You

accomplish that with a message, a story, and a brand that gets people excited and fired up. Think about it: How many BAD presentations have you sat through before? Hundreds right? Well I work with you to create a presentation experience that your audience will never forget and establishes you as an expert in your field, a person that people want to work with, and different from everyone else who does what you do. No matter the area you want to work on, I educate you, I liberate you from the dead end practices that are not getting the results you want, and I entertain you in the process because I know feeling like you are sitting back in the classroom being lectured at is not a fun way to spend your valuable time! Let's work hard but have fun doing it!"

The above example is about sixty to ninety seconds long and works well when you are introducing yourself to someone for the first time. If you go to any networking events where everyone has a turn at their elevator speech, you know how challenging it can be to "effortlessly" present yourself in a way that resonates with other people.

Before you get to work on your answer, consider the following suggestions:

1. CONCRETE LANGUAGE
Strive for the most concrete language you can find. "We maximize shareholder value," is just a lot of mumbo jumbo and people tend to tune out when they hear this kind of talk. Compare this example:

"I am in marketing"

versus

"I align your message with the right audience,
I help you simplify your messaging about your product/service,
and I show you how to launch campaigns that get results."

2. USE EXAMPLES
People respond well to examples and they serve as valuable proof of your credibility.

3. PROVIDE EVIDENCE
Add evidence to your statement. Use the above example of a marketing professional, and add this statement as evidence.

"I recently finished a project with Bliss Spa and Salon. In just 90 days we grew their Facebook fan page with 1500 new likes, launched a Spring product and service special with an email and direct mail campaign, and the salon saw a 40% increase in new client appointments."

4. PRACTICE

Don't wait until you are in a situation where you are called upon to answer the question "what do you bring to the table?" Take the time to get your response down pat and strive to be conversational in your answer. Practice now so you will knock their socks off when it is the real deal!

Use the following to begin designing your answer to "What do you bring to the table?"

WHO I Am:

WHAT I DO:

THIS IS WHY IT MATTERS:

Congratulations! You are on your way to finding your Plan Be! You are ready for Activity #7 where you will lay out your Plan Be in full. Are you ready? I am. Let's get it done.

*You may be wondering what I "bring to the table" for family gatherings. That's easy: Sonic Ice. It's my specialty.

You're off to Great Places! Today is your day! Your mountain is waiting, So... get on your way!

Dr. Seuss

Activity #7:
Your Plan Be

Wow. We have completed six activities and now your Plan Be should start to come into focus. Are you feeling the calorie burn from all the brain exercising? Me too! We are ready to put your plan on paper using the work you have completed so far, and adding to it with some short term and long term planning.

For quite some time I have harbored a fantasy I want to share with you. I want a vegetable garden. (Were you hoping for something a little more risque? Shame on you!) I did some "digging" (yes the pun is intended) today using Pinterest Gardening, and came across a lovely website called Smart Gardener. Now, this is my kind of website! While I have wanted to have a vegetable garden for a very long time, I never really knew how to get started. I feel intimidated by the prospect of growing my own vegetables because I am not someone who has a green thumb. Whenever I bring a new plant home my husband says, "Oh you poor little plant. You are not long for this world."

> "Most men die at 25...we just don't bury them until they are 70."
> Benjamin Franklin

Smart Gardener was probably designed for people like me: Good intentions, but lacks that real knowledge to be successful. Yep. That's me! Their tag line is Plant, Grow, Harvest (three words by the way), and I love the simplicity of this idea. When you get started on Smart Gardener you put in your zip code, and they recommend to you the kinds of plants you can grow in your region based on climate, soil, etc. Using other criteria, you can also tell the website the kinds of vegetables, fruits, and herbs you are interested in. From there your virtual garden begins to take shape so that you can manifest that garden in your own space. Real space. Real vegetables. Real fruit. Real herbs. Real hungry.

I have only gotten as far as the website (I am going to have to talk my hubba hubba into helping me with this project), so you will have to check in with me later and see if I followed through on this intention I have set. But I did speak it into the universe, and then I found a beautiful website that would show me how to not only plant my little garden, but will send me daily, weekly, monthly, and seasonal emails to tell me what I should be doing with my garden. It's kind of like gardening for dummies. And I am the dummy.

What do you want to plant, grow, and harvest? A new career perhaps? The courage to move to a new state? What about going back to school to complete a degree, or ending something you have outgrown a long time ago? Whatever it is that you want to achieve, realize, pursue, or change in your life, I hope Plan Be will give you the language and structure to not only get started, but to realize this goal.

From point A to point Be! That is where we are headed. Let's talk about how to get there.

Come January, millions upon millions of people make their New Year resolutions, and if we are to believe the statistics, most people abandon these resolutions before the calendar reaches February 1st. Why? One of the primary reasons is people lack a structure or process to work within. The concept of finding your Plan Be is to give you a strategy to not only find your plan for success, but to reach it because you did the work up front and you built in the steps to get there.

Whether you start in January or choose to start today, Plan Be is available to you for both short term and long term success planning. It can be used for your personal life, or your professional life. Plan Be will work in planning for your team or department and it can be applied at a grander level to your entire organization. Plan Be is a plan, a strategy, a program, and a language to use in realizing success.

In my own mind, Plan Be is like having a GPS to direct you, but it allows you to also use your eyes, ears, and intuition. Both are necessary and good in goal setting. GPS will give you the step-by-step instructions to get to your destination, but if you rely on GPS 100%, you might miss other "signs" and "signals" that tell you to slow down, look around, consider a different path, and sometimes abandon ship. Your own experience, intuition, and perceptiveness will play a key role in realizing your true success story. I want you to pay attention to these things too. Imagine for a moment that you are headed to the Grand Canyon, a destination you have dreamt about seeing your whole life.

You plug in the address (does the Grand Canyon have an address?) on your GPS, get in the drivers seat, and set out on your path to arrive at the Grand Canyon. But, what if, along the way, you miss out on other points of interest you did not even know were out there to stop and see, experience, and enjoy? That is where your own internal GPS kicks in. It keeps you alert to other things along the way to your ultimate destination. Your "internal GPS" keeps you open to experiencing things that life puts in your path that you might otherwise ignore when you are operating on auto-pilot.

Before we dive in, let's review the first six activities using earlier examples and bring them all together at one time so you can reference each of them as your build your Plan Be.

Here are my answers to each of the six activities:

My THREE words:
educate | liberate | entertain

My No No List:

1. Don't handle other's people's money.
2. Paperwork, filling out forms, etc.
3. Editing my own work.
4. Housekeeping on a weekly basis.
5. Volunteering for things that involve a lot of kids at one time.

My Lizard Brain tells me and I respond to it with:

"You are a fraud."
"You don't know what you are doing."
"You are going to fail and everyone is going to tell the whole world what an idiot you are."
"Why would anyone listen to you?"

"Hi there lizard brain. I know what you are up to and I am not playing with you today!"

"I have something to share with the world, and they will be better for having heard it."

"I have done my work. I am prepared. I know what I am talking about."

Break Rules

Plan A says:	I say:
Your job comes first.	I WILL have balance, and family comes first. Period.
Titles Matter.	I don't care about titles and don't use them.
Tell your client what they want to hear	I speak the truth to my clients even if it makes me nervous. I know it is the right thing to do.
Do everything!	I will specialize instead of trying to do it all!
Always say YES!	Say No with courage and confidence.
Women nod their head and keep the peace.	Face conflict. Manage it like an adult. Don't avoid it.

Plan A says:	I say:
Work is Work.	Work is fun.
Manage your children's lives like a boss	Give my kids the tools they need to manage their lives. Be there when they need me. Don't micromanage.
Check your kids grades daily.	My kids grades are their responsibility, not mine.
If you work hard enough, and want it bad enough you can have it all.	Having it all is stupid and a waste of a good life. I can't have it all, and more importantly I don't want to have it all. I will prioritize what matters most to me and not let anyone tell me what should matter.

Be my own dictionary.

My definition for success for the next seven years looks like this:

1. Earn a steady income as a consultant who trains and educates my clients to be better communicators so they can stand out in the marketplace.
2. Maintain a 60/40 split between training projects and keynote speaking.
3. Be home to take my girls to school and pick them up when school gets out at least three or four days out of the week. Coordinate my schedule with my husband's so he can be home to take and pick up when I can't.
4. Be home during the summer where I can work from home and have at least one "play day" during the week to go to the pool, go to Six Flags, go shopping, and just hang out with my kids.
5. Take two vacations a year with my husband and girls.
6. Take one vacation a year with my husband.
7. Have time to raise money for the What's Your Plan Be? Scholarship Fund.
8. Make time in my calendar to give back to the United Way of Denton County.
9. Serve on the board of the Denton Public Schools Foundation.
10. Go to lunch with a girlfriend during the week if the occasion presents itself.

What do you bring to the table?

In my professional life: I provide a unique learning experience that teaches my client to implement communication best practices that allow them to stand out in a noisy and crowded marketplace. I am honest, direct, great at strategizing, and brainstorming. I bring creative ideas to the table.

In my personal life: I am a great mom and wife who is accessible to my family. I provide an ear to listen to friends and family who just need someone to talk to. I love to entertain my family and friends with stories and jokes. Making them laugh is my spiritual gift and it fills my cup. I love hosting beautiful events. I love entertaining people in my own home and being the perfect hostess.

Take the time to bring your activities together on one or two pages. Grab a few blank sheets of paper and get to work, or if you are like me and you type faster than you write, get your computer out and get to work.

Now that you have all your activities together, we are ready to begin identify your Plan Be. To do that, please answer the following questions. Find a quiet spot where you can think clearly and without interruption. Don't judge your answers or begin generating a list of all the reasons your answers are stupid, little, unrealistic, or selfish. Repeat this three times before you begin:

I will be kind to myself.
I will allow myself the space to find my Plan Be.
I want to be more of what I was put here to do.

Answer the following questions:

1. What do you lay in bed at night and fantasize about? What dream do you harbor but share with no one else?

2. What would you pursue if there were no obstacles in front of you?

3. If you were to pursue this what would you have to give up to make it happen?

4. Where do you get "high" in your life? (the activity where you are in the zone)

5. What three things do you know you can do to make your dream happen?

In our recent move, I came across a box filled with my old day timers from college. Every fall semester I would purchase a new Texas Tech University academic calendar/planner, and I would get to work on organizing my days. I LIVED around what was in this planner. Without it, I am certain I would not have been able to function. Looking through these planners, it was a treat to read them. They were almost like a diary of my life--where I was every day, what I was doing, and what was important to me. School, work, and my social life, all written down on the pages of these planners for me to see. I thought my life was highly complicated at that time and this planner was what held my world together. Little did I know that life was not nearly as complex and complicated in those days where all I had to worry about was me, myself, and I.

Today I have a lot more on my plate. Naming, claiming, and living my Plan Be is situated around the reality of my life:

TEN THINGS ABOUT MY LIFE: THE GOOD AND THE CHALLENGING

1. I have a husband who travels for work.
2. I travel for work.
3. I have 13 and 11 year old daughters who are social and involved in activities. That means that I am a chauffeur a lot of the time!
4. I am a small business owner with an assistant who works ten hours a week for me.
5. I have a wonderful support system of family and friends, especially my mother in law, who is always happy to help out when we need her!
6. My husband parents with me and does a lot to allow me to be a mom who works. We take turns on a lot of things and that is a BIG help.
7. I live in a major metroplex and that is advantageous in so many ways but especially as a business owner--there will always be work here for me.
8. I am very connected to the business community where I live, and have built a business support system for myself over the last five years.
9. I am not well connected to the Dallas business community but I am working on it!
10. My children are older and more independent these days which allows me some flexibility in my schedule.

TEN THINGS ABOUT ME: THE GOOD AND THE CHALLENGING

1. I am VERY easily distracted in my day-to-day life.
2. I am a dreamer. At any given moment I may be hatching thirteen different ways to rule the world.
3. I can get caught up in other people's dreams too, and lose focus on what I am working on.
4. I compare my "success" to the success of those who do what I do,and often feel like I am not measuring up.
5. I LOVE learning and can get absorbed in the reading and research part of my job when I should be doing other things.
6. I am always going to go after what I want. I don't let fear stop me. I can lead with my emotions at the start, but I believe that if I spend too much time analyzing I will never get anything done.
7. I love winning. Landing a new client, a new speaking gig, or selling a book--all these things feel like a win and it gets me high.
8. I am self motivated. I don't need a cheerleader on the sidelines pushing me (although it is always good to have encouragement) because I will get myself there.
9. I am not afraid to ask for anything. I like the challenge of getting people to say yes.
10. I am a VERY social person with loner tendencies. Does that make sense? I know it's weird. I love people and being around people but I also need my alone time.

Clearly, what's on my plate is a smidge more than what I dealt with as a college student! Life is busy, frustrating, stressful. wonderful, adventurous, and messy. Life is good. In the midst of these things, my Plan Be gives me the focus and determination to live the kind of life I envision for myself. I don't want my dream life to be more exciting than my real life, but I do know that the kind of life I want for myself will not happen on it's own. I must be willing to do the hard work.

Take a moment on the next page and complete the same activity for yourself.

TEN THINGS ABOUT MY LIFE: THE GOOD AND THE CHALLENGING

1.

2.

3.

4.

5.

6.

7.

8.

9.

10.

TEN THINGS ABOUT ME: THE GOOD AND THE CHALLENGING

1.

2.

3.

4.

5.

6.

7.

8.

9.

10.

Naming, claiming, and living your Plan Be requires that you be upfront and honest with yourself about where you are at right here and now in your life. The more audacious the Plan Be you set, the more work it will require of you to get there. If you are not willing or ready to do the work then start with something smaller that will get you on your way.

The next step in the process is to name your Plan Be. Set a timer for three minutes and on a piece of paper write down the things you want in your life. Here are some prompts you can use to help generate your list.

1. What do you want to feel more of in your life?
2. What things make you feel "high"?
3. What is something you did at one time and you loved it, but over the years you have quit doing it?
4. Where are areas in your life that you are not showing up but know you need to?
5. What things do you want for yourself personally?
6. What things do you want for yourself professionally?

If you do well by seeing an example, let me share my own answers to these questions:

1. I want to feel balanced and full of energy. I want to feel like I am making a difference in my community. I want to feel the satisfaction of hard work. I want to feel happy and healthy. I want to feel rested. I want to feel connected to my family and friends. I want to feel passionate about the things that matter to me. I want to feel compassionate.

2. I get high when: I give a presentation, teach a class, work with a group of people who care about the things I care about too, travel and eat good food, make choices that will benefit my future self, push through something that is hard for me to do, meet new people.

3. I love playing tennis but quit about two years ago and I would like to get back to it.

4. My health. I don't get enough sleep, I put off doctor's appointments, I need to lose weight so all my clothes fit. I don't always show up with my family either. We may be in the same space, but very often I am preoccupied with other things. I need to spend more time giving them my full attention.

5. In my personal life I want to have the freedom to spend time with my girls and my husband on the weekends. I want to be able to take a three day weekend every once in a while. I want to have the freedom to go to lunch with a girlfriend during the week. I want to be able to spend time nurturing friendships. I want to

spend time at home making my home a lovely sanctuary. I want to host parties and invite our friends to our home.

6. In my professional life I want to earn an income that will allow me contribute to our monthly budget, put back money for our retirement, help our girls pay for college, take two vacations a year, and eventually be debt free. I want to continue to grow my "footprint" across Texas and the United States adding new clients to my portfolio every year. I want to improve the quality of my product year in and year out. I want to make enough money that Bravo cc will eventually contribute money every year to the WYPB Scholarships for Girls fund.

Look at your own list and try to come up with Be statements based on your answers. Here is what my list looks like:

Be BALANCED	Be ENERGIZED	Be CONNECTED
Be A TEACHER	Be PASSIONATE	Be WELL FED
Be WELL TRAVELED	Be COMMITTED	Be HEALTHY
Be ACTIVE	Be PRESENT FOR MY FAMILY	
Be FREE	Be A FINANCIAL CONTRIBUTOR	
Be GENEROUS		

Please notice my Be list says nothing about my weight or making a million dollars in 48 hours. I am not discouraging you from either of these areas, but instead I want you to think about them differently. If you consider my list from above, you will see that several of my Plan Be statements will ultimately impact the scale for me. If I am healthy and active, I can't help but reap the rewards of watching the number go down on the scale. My focus is on something fundamentally more important than my weight. It is on my quality of life.

The same can be said for issues of $$$$$$$. Money is great. I love what it can do and the experiences it has allowed me to have in my life. More money means more options, and it also means I can do more in the world to make the world a happier place. With all that being said, putting my FOCUS on money as part of my Plan Be just does not jive for me. I spend a lot of time on Facebook because it is a business tool I use to stay connected to my audience. The number of posts that show up in my feed daily about making money baffle me. Reading these posts make me feel dirty. I cannot stand the emphasis that is placed on "six figure income working just 10 hours a week" or "learn the 14 steps I used to make $30,000 in just 5 minutes" mindset is not for me. So if Be RICH is your plan, you will likely be disappointed with my philosophy.

Here is the way I synthesize my position on these two issues: skinny + money. No one on their death bed says to their family and friends at their bedside, "I sure do wish I had been skinnier and had more money."

Agreed?

You have named your Plan Be. The next part of the process is claiming it! You are far more likely to live out your Plan Be when you make a proclamation to yourself and the world that you are on this journey. What does Claim It! look like? First and foremost, I want you to put your Plan Be somewhere that you will see it daily. Start with some Post It Notes and a marker. Write down your Plan Be and put it on your bathroom mirror and fridge. These are two places you are likely to visit every day. Think of two other places you can put your Plan Be to remind yourself of how you are going to live your life: Your car or computer monitor is an idea. Maybe your nightstand is somewhere you look every day. How about on your desk at work? Just the act of writing our your Plan Be and then putting it in places that you will SEE daily is a move in the right direction.

After you have completed this step, I want you to share it with two to three people who will help keep you focused. One of my new training topics this year that has been unexpectedly popular is accountability. Sharing your Plan Be with other people who will hold you accountable is going to help you be successful. Prompt them on ways they can encourage you when you are doing a great job and ideas on how to redirect you when you get off course. Give them PERMISSION to redirect you so that they feel comfortable providing this kind of feedback.

You have staked your claim so let's get to living your Plan Be. I encourage you to think of ways you can LIVE your Plan Be:

Daily

Weekly

Monthly

Yearly

Make a list of the REAL things you can do to achieve the Be statements you generated. Start with THREE Be statements that are most timely to you in your life right now. Your statements need to be as specific as possible so that you will know if you met the goal of not. Consider:

"I will get enough sleep every night"

versus

"I will go to bed by 10:30m during the week and be asleep by 11:00pm"

Clearly, the second option is superior to the first. It is specific and measurable. You either did it or you didn't do it. When you choose vague language to name your goal it is much easier to miss the mark or fool yourself into thinking you met the goal when you really didn't.

Now...

1. Take four clean, white pieces of paper and at the top of the page label them Daily, Weekly, Monthly, Yearly.
2. Note ways on each of these four sheets you can live your Plan Be with specific action items. Aim for three to five items per list, any more than that and you are likely to become overwhelmed.
3. Take pictures of your lists and keep them in your smart phone so you can reference them.
4. Send your list to the person or persons who have agreed to help you stay accountable.
5. Schedule ONE HOUR every week on the same day and same time that you will spend looking over your list and assessing your progress. Be ready to re-route if something is not working.
6. Take your original lists and put them somewhere that you will see them daily. If you have a home office or work office that you work from daily, this is a good spot for these lists.

Congratulations! You have designed a Plan Be for your life that gives you direction on what to do daily, weekly, monthly, and annually. That was the easy work. The real work is the day-to-day effort to live your plan. You know that most people fail to meet their goals. You may fall into that category as well. The reasons are a long, laundry list of excuses, blaming, Lizard brain talk, and more.

I hope now you have a process that will allow you to live the kind of life that you have been dreaming of. The last step is to Plan to Fail. Read on to understand why in the world I would ask you to plan your own failure.

Failures are finger posts
on the road to achievement.

C.S. Lewis

Activity #8:
Plan to Fail

Q: How do you eat an elephant?

A: One bite at a time.

In our hurry up and get there culture, where our attention span is about a nanosecond these days, the ability to stick with it can be daunting. We have all heard of the recent college graduate at her first "real" job asking, after just three months, "When will I get a promotion?" It would be easy to feel exasperated and frustrated by this mindset but let's be honest: We all could use a little help in the waiting department. We want it now dang it!

In this landscape of the 24-hour news cycle, instant access to anything and everything at all times of the day, an overabundance of technology at our fingertips, and the traffic jammed information highway that we are becoming a culture of people who have little concept of what it means to "pay your dues" by earning things the old fashioned way: Through hard work, sweat, tears, and TIME.

A 2004 article in *Psychology Today* suggests this new and modern age will live in is producing a generation of wimps. This intriguing and challenging article struck a chord when I shared it on Facebook one Sunday afternoon. Like a wildfire blazing through the West Texas Plains, my Facebook friends began sharing the post with their network. One of my favorite observations in the article includes how children view life today:

> You get used to things happening right away. You not only want the pizza now, you generalize that expectation to other domains, like friendship and intimate relationships. You become frustrated and impatient easily. You become unwilling to work out problems. And so relationships fail—perhaps the single most powerful experience leading to depression. http://www.psychologytoday.com/articles/200411/nation-wimps

This reality is not limited to those under the age of 18. In fact, I see it among adults too. I am guilty myself of having my smart phone in hand non stop when I should be focused on what is happening around me.

Shawn Parr, the Guvner & CEO of Bulldog Drummond, an innovation and design consultancy headquartered in San Diego, in an article for *Fast Company,* argues that our obsession with the smart phone is turning us all into idiots. He points out the warning signs in the following list:

Warning Signs that you are becoming an IDIOT:

Do you look at your emails from your phone in bed?

Do you take your phone to the bathroom?

Do you DWT (Drive While Texting)?

Do you jump between email, the news, project documents, Facebook, Instagram, and Twitter?

Do you eat dinner with your family with your phone in your hand?

Do you compulsively check to see if you have new messages and LIKES on your latest post?

Do you post everything you do, every moment of the day?

Do you go out for dinner and midway through take photos of what you're eating and post them immediately?

Do you go out for dinner and spend more time looking at your phone than your date?

Do you sit in a meeting and check your phone every few minutes?

http://www.fastcompany.com/3012432/creative-conversations/are-you-an-idiot

On almost every one of the items in Parr's list, I am guilty of this idiot behavior. It's embarrassing. It's shameful. I know that I am not making the world a better place for my girls when I am always "plugged in" to technology. These modern day "conveniences" make the process of setting goals and achieving them that much more difficult because we have lost our sense of wait time. But there is something to be said for waiting and earning it, isn't there? When my daughter saves her money and buys something she wanted me to buy but I said no, it is that much more satisfying to her that she saved her money and bought it herself. I know because she told me so! One of those rare parenting moments when you think, "Maybe I am doing something right!"

Naming, claiming, and living your Plan Be is something that gives you room to grow. It does not have to happen in one fail swoop and you won't lose ten pounds in 48 hours or make $100,000 by the end of the week (unless you would like to sell me your kidney). Plan Be is not a place where you arrive one day and proclaim "I graduated! I am done. The work is over!" Plan Be is not a destination, it is a journey. To go on that journey, I want you to spend a few minutes and PLAN TO FAIL.

"Fail? I have done all this work and you are asking me to Plan to Fail? That's not cool!"

I understand but....my reasons have merit. By planning how you will fail (and fail big!), you are far more likely to be successful.

Ask yourself, "What conditions, characteristics, and circumstances are going to get in the way of my success?"

Choose from the following "usual suspects":

Shifting priorities

Over scheduled days, weeks, months

Committing to things you don't care about

Procrastination

Fear

Discouragement from the vampires in your life

Excuse making

Drama

Refusing to ask for help

Trying to do all things for all people all the time

Worry

Getting caught up in other people's dreams

Lack of rest

Bad habits

Shame/Guilt

Belief that you don't deserve good things

Martyr Syndrome

Lack of focus, too easily distracted

Wasting time

Choosing instant gratification in favor of long term wins

I would be willing to be that at different times in your life, you have allowed about 75% of the items on this list to sabotage your success. I certainly know that I have struggled and continue to struggle with some of these items. We all have been there, and if you are anything like me, it can be a daily challenge to make the right decisions that get me closer to living out my own Plan Be.

In Plan to Fail, you are going to set up strategies from the beginning of your journey to deal with these self destructive qualities from the beginning. If you are a parent, do you take an emergency kit with you when traveling with the kids for summer vacation? Yes, of course you do! Why? Because you know that there may be a few bumps, bruises, and scrapes on your vacation adventure. In Plan to Fail, you are doing the same thing. You don't hope for bumps, bruises, and scrapes, but you know through experience that it is better to plan for the worst.

What are FIVE things you can do today, tomorrow, and in the weeks to come to resist the urge to self sabotage your Plan Be? Here is my own list that will help you get started.

Shifting Priorities
I will start each week by making a list of the 7 to 10 things I will accomplish that week. These will be the things I work on until completion. When a new idea comes to me, I will put it in my idea file and not do anything with it until I have completed my priority list for the week.

Lack of Rest
I will be in bed by 10:30pm every night during the week and asleep by 11:00pm. I will plug my phone in to charge in the bathroom so I can't reach for it and check my email.

Procrastination
I will spend the first 45 minutes of my morning doing the things I hate to do and get them off my plate so I can focus the rest of my day on the things that fill my cup.

Lack of Focus, Too Easily Distracted
I will set alarms on my phone in 45 minute increments where I will work on one thing without interruption. I will put my phone on silent and let calls go to voice mail. I will close down all open tabs on my computer desktop. I will find a quiet place to work.

Over scheduled days, weeks, months
I will set my work hours at the beginning of the day and step away from the computer and all work at the end of my work day. I will ALWAYS check my calendar before I say yes to an event. I will keep one day open during the week to attend to personal things on my to-do list versus doing these things randomly. I will share my schedule with my husband so that we don't have any misunderstandings.

If you struggle to identify the ways that you "get in the way" of your own success then consider asking someone to tell you. This can be painful, but necessary if you don't really know how you self sabotage. Choose someone you know who loves you and cares about your success, and be specific in your request. My good friend, Melissa Cox, is the kind of friend I would ask this question. She is kind, and I know she wants the best for me. I might say something like this:

"Melissa, I just read this book on finding your Plan Be and I really liked the ideas in it. I have identified three things I want to Be and I was hoping you could give me some feedback on things you have noticed about me where I might have a tendency to self sabotage."

Don't stop there.

"Melissa, can you give me an example of a past situation where you saw me self sabotage?"

And then be quiet.

And listen.

And say, "Thank you," when this person gives you feedback.

Resist the urge to argue, prove them wrong, or become defensive.

The next step you take to Plan to Fail is building in inspiration and future learning to keep you on track. What follows are my own recommendations on the best and brightest people out there.

INSPIRATION & ENCOURAGEMENT

DANIELLE LAPORTE | www.daniellelaporte.com
I recommend Danielle to everyone. She is honest, funny, challenging, and REAL. I love this lady and feel like we are girlfriends (we have never met but I think we will one day!).

ELIZABETH GILBERT | www.elizabethgilbert.com
To say that Gilbert's book *Eat, Pray, Love* changed my life would be an understatement. No kidding. When I read her book seven years ago I was dumbstruck by her courage, tenacity, and sense of humor about life. Gilbert gets the "big so what?" and I continue to reach for her book when I need to remind myself of what I am working on.

MESSAGING

SETH GODIN | www.sethgodin.com

I recommend Seth to anyone who needs further instruction on marketing and messaging. There are A LOT of "experts" out there in the world of marketing but Seth is one of the few who can confidently wear the title of expert. His books are beyond fantastic and there are many to choose from. In the context of finding and living out your Plan Be, I recommend you start with *Linchpin*.

PRESENTATION/PUBLIC SPEAKING

GARR REYNOLDS | www.garrreynolds.com

NANCY DUARTE | www.duarte.com

SLIDESHARE | www.slideshare.net

You are on your way! Can you feel it? I hope you can, and I hope it feels good. Like pretzels with chocolate and a big glass of really cold milk kind of good. The remainder of this book explores a sample Plan Be that is common among the professionals I work with across industries, business types, and professions: The old dreaded public speaking.

I chose to outline this Plan Be because it is a subject matter that is near and dear to my heart. I am a true believer when it comes to the power of a presentation. Every person can benefit from learning how to present their ideas, opinions, experiences, story, and expertise through a presentation.

Be a Presentation Super Hero is meant to serve as an extended example of how to use the activities we have detailed so far.

Your Plan Be can be a plan that works on your strengths (Your Three Words) or it can be a plan to work on areas where you know you need to experience growth, but it does not come naturally to you.

We need both kinds of Plan Be's. I have found over the years that people have a tendency to either spend all their time on the good "stuff" or spend all the time on the bad "stuff."

Well, I am asking you to spend time on both the good and the bad. You must actively seek out ways to explore avenues for growth in both areas of your life.

Whether public speaking is a strength or a weakness for you, I am certain you will enjoy seeing for yourself how you can implement what you have learned.

Grab your cape and get ready to tap into your Presentation Super Hero powers!

"According to most studies,
people's number one fear is public speaking.
Number two is death.
Death is number two.
Does that sound right?
This means to the average person,
if you go to a funeral,
you're better off in the casket
than doing the eulogy."

Jerry Seinfeld

BE A PRESENTATION SUPERHERO

The first time I got high, I was seven years old.

My family took a road trip vacation from Lubbock, Texas, to California. My sisters were 13 and 17, and I was 7. We did not travel in a pimped out Suburban complete with television, DVD player, hot tub, wet bar, and valet (You know: How our kids travel these days). No, we traveled in my mom's four-door, blue chevrolet. I am not sure if seat belts were mandatory in 1980, but I don't remember wearing one, and my sweet father had fashioned me a bed in the floorboard of the backseat where I could nap and my sisters would have more room in the actual seat. Ah...sweet memories.

This trip was the trip of a lifetime for a seven-year old. It would be my first time to visit California, my first time to visit Disneyland, Universal Studios, and a real bona fide California Beach. But what I remember most is our day at an in-studio taping for a new game show.

Now, if you have never been to a game show taping, they send out a comedian beforehand to warm up the audience. After about twenty minutes our comedian ran out of material and made an offer to let someone from the audience come up and tell a joke.

> You could be Ivy League educated, well read, and off the charts smart, **but it doesn't matter if you can't connect to people with your words.**

Up went my hand!

My sisters both sighed heavily, rolled their eyes, and asked my mom to please make me sit down. But the comedian had already made eye contact with me, and he chose ME! I had been waiting for this moment my whole life.

Up I went, and I proceeded to tell a joke my sister Lauren had told me a few weeks earlier. I don't remember the joke, but I do remember the punchline. The kid says to his teacher "I'm Superman!"

What I remember vividly is that the crowd roared their approval after I told my joke with clapping, shouting, bravos, and more!

What happened next is a moment that defined my life and my destiny.

The comedian pulled out a ten dollar bill and handed it to me. It was my first paid gig as a speaker! An older gentleman in the audience called out, "Give her more!" It was in that freeze frame, *Chariots of Fire* moment, that I realized--I can get paid to do this! And today I do.

I have never done illegal drugs in my life. Heck, I have never smoked a cigarette. But I get high all the time. It started that day in California, 33 years ago. At seven years old I learned my gift, and it was public speaking. My whole life I have gravitated to the stage, and if there is a microphone in the general area, watch out because I am going to try and get my hands on it!

With the popularity of American Idol and other singing competitions, I wondered-- what speaker would WIN an American Idol type contest for the greatest speaker in America? One thing led to another, and I found myself Googling "Greatest speeches of all time," and naturally there were thousands of hits. What I found so interesting was the different kinds of "Greatest speeches" out there: Political, Commencement, Religious, Humorous, Oscar Acceptance, Sports, Business, etc. So many speeches, so little time. The take away is simple: Speeches, no matter their purpose or audience, are powerful. So powerful that I need only say, "I have a dream," to you, and you are instantly moved. Changed. Inspired.

The goal of this chapter is to illustrate for you how you can become a Presentation Super Hero. To get you started, stop for a moment and think about the GREATEST speech you have ever heard.

> The spoken word can move people. **The collective experience of an audience and speaker has changed history throughout the centuries.**

Mentally note a few reasons WHY it was such an amazing speech. How did it make you feel? What impact did it have on you? What do you still remember today about that speech?

The power of the spoken word cannot be underestimated. Great men and women alike have captivated and MOVED people to action with their eloquence. This truth is the reason I have a job. People recognize how important it is to be able to articulate their thoughts and ideas to others in a meaningful way, but the actual implementation of this job can befuddle even the best and brightest.

I think it is important to define what I mean by Be a Presentation Super Hero. Essentially I want you to find your inner presenter. I want you to be articulate. Articulate for me is NOT about your ability to speak over people's heads, quote esoteric passages from great thinkers from our past, or drone on and on and on. (As I kid I remember sitting through a prayer at church one Sunday evening that lasted more than ten minutes. And it was a painful ten minutes indeed.) Being articulate is about connecting to other people with your words. Those who are truly articulate are able to illuminate ideas in a way that inspires us to act, change, or reconsider. There is nothing fake or manufactured about being articulate. No cookie cutter messages will do.

Charisma does not require that one be loud, gregarious, or larger than life. It simply requires that you be

REAL.

To some degree being articulate is about charisma. But charisma comes in many different flavors. It is easy to see the charisma found in someone like Steve Jobs when he took the stage dressed in his typical black turtleneck and jeans, but at the same time Warren Buffett and his home spun charm is also charismatic. **Charisma is simple. It comes from a place of TRUTH and HONESTY.** It is where passion reveals itself. Charisma does not require that one be loud, gregarious, or larger than life. It simply requires that you be real.

A few years back a successful executive in the beverage distribution industry called me for help with an upcoming presentation he would be doing in front of his industry peers at a national level conference. This presentation was important for his career and his credibility. He knew that this presentation would reflect not only on him, but on his organization as well.

Upon arriving to work with him for the first time, I learned that he was a graduate of Harvard Business School. Harvard. Business. School. Note to self: It does not matter how well educated you are, or the quality of institution you were schooled at, being well-spoken is an art form that takes work for everyone. Lucky for me, it turned out that he had great potential to speak and captivate his audience. His greatest challenge was quieting his Lizard brain--that voice in your head that tells you, "You aren't smart enough. People will laugh at you. They won't take you seriously. Why should anyone listen to you?"

After getting his Lizard brain to pipe down, we tackled his presentation style and put his slides in their place, and he was ready. I am happy to report that after his successful presentation one of his team members emailed me and told me that his presentation had a warm and enthusiastic reception.

Being articulate matters. This is why presidents have speech writers. I have said for years that if I could pass one law it would be this: If you run for political office or are elected to political office you MUST, by law, write your own speeches. (My second law would be that if you throw a cigarette butt from your car window or as you are walking, you will be shot on sight. Tough? Yes. But I think it would result in a 0% rate of people throwing their cigarettes down.) I am not interested in hearing someone speak another person's words. What does that demonstrate? Anyone can do that. My school-aged daughters can do that.

I want to listen to someone tell me their own original thoughts and ideas. Your ability to talk about complex issues and ideas is a demonstration of your knowledge about these very things. Being well spoken is a testimony to your ability to engage in critical thinking.

Should the measure of a person's competence be judged by their ability to articulate? Well, yes, it should. Being smart is not good enough. If you can't COMMUNICATE your ideas, your thoughts, your service, your product, and your vision to other people in a way that they say, "I want some of what he's got!" then fo-get-about-it. You could be Ivy League educated, well read, and off the charts smart, but it doesn't matter if you can't connect to people with your words.

Let's go back to politics for a moment. When historians reflect on high stakes elections like the presidential race and attempt to determine why one candidate prevails over the other, their public speaking prowess is often an item of consideration. The 1960 televised debates between John F. Kennedy and Richard Nixon are perhaps the most infamous illustration. In September of 2010, *Time* magazine went so far as to say that the televised Nixon-Kennedy debate changed the world. Wow! That is a bold statement.

Media Historian, Alan Schroeder, notes about the Kennedy-Nixon debate, "It's one of those unusual points on the timeline of history where you can say things changed very dramatically — in this case, in a single night." What had changed was the way American citizens interfaced with their candidates. Before televised debates, candidates came to their citizenry by way of newspaper or radio programs. But in 1960, things changed and that night the play book by which a candidate gets elected was forever changed. Being articulate mattered again (Remember the famous Lincoln-Douglas debates?).

Today, one of the criteria by which an individual is even considered for a campaign run is how they will play in front of an audience (Code for "is this person articulate?"). Larry Sabato, political analyst at the University of Virginia, observes, "When parties are considering their candidates, they ask: Who would look better on TV? Who comes across better? Who can debate better? This has been taken into the calculus."

Fast forward a few years and plug in the formula.

Ronald Reagan versus Jimmy Carter and Walter Mondale:

Ronald Reagan will forever be known as, "The Great Communicator." His communication style was such that the every-day Joe felt that Reagan understood him. Lou Cannon, a White House correspondent during the Reagan Presidency, captured Reagan's essence in a piece written for *USA Today* after his death. He writes so eloquently:

> Reagan became the great communicator because he stood for something. In 1980, when Reagan ran for president, he talked more about issues than any presidential candidate had in years. He talked about building up the defense budget, cutting taxes and balancing the budget. Former House member John Anderson (an independent presidential candidate that year) said the only way you can do the three of them was with mirrors. But Reagan did two of the three. So he talked about substance. But he kept his message basic and simple and on mainstream American concerns.

Other candidates didn't have a chance against him when it came to the ability to capture and captivate an audience--just ask Jimmy Carter and Walter Mondale.

Bob Dole versus Bill Clinton:

Throughout Dole's bid to be elected president, he showed a lack of charisma at every turn. To most people, he came across as a stodgy, cantankerous, old guy. He was wooden and defensive with reporters and voters. Amazingly, AFTER losing his bid for the presidency, he went on David Letterman and revealed he had a PERSONALITY! He was engaging, funny, honest, and most importantly he was human! Why did he not show this part of himself in the campaign? Who knows? Clinton, on the other hand, was spot on as a candidate. He had a special way of making someone on the other side of the television FEEL like he was speaking directly to them. Charisma and eloquence clearly played a key role in this election.

George W. Bush versus Al Gore:

Let's be honest here. Neither of these guys are giants when it comes to being articulate. In fact, in my own estimation, George W. Bush is one of the most inarticulate presidents we have had in the last fifty years. But...when compared to Al Gore during the actual election, he won the battle over who was perceived as the better communicator. Bush may not be a great speaker, but at least he had some charisma going for him. For many people, he was highly likable and his "aw shucks" charm went a long way. Al Gore, on the other hand, had neither charisma or charm. He came across as distant and academic. He managed to alienate potential voters with his lack of personality.

We could detail a long list of political characters, but you understand my point here. Being articulate matters. Like it or not--this is true in every walk of life and will remain true forever. No matter your profession, you will be judged by the words that come out of your mouth. If you say "strategery" instead of "strategy," don't be surprised when people refuse to let it go.

Your lack of articulation can be your undoing as well. In one of 2010's most viral videos, GOP hopeful, Phil Davison, of Minvera, Ohio, learned this lesson the hard way. If you haven't seen the video go to You Tube and Google Phil Davison, and watch his meltdown captured on camera.

Contain your laughter, and let's break down the video. In short, Phil loses his mind. In just five minutes, he takes the Howard Dean primal scream and multiplies it by 1000. As it turns out, Phil is multi-degreed, with two Master's degrees (One of them in communication studies!), and in front of God and everyone he lost his mind. His meltdown garnered national attention from the blogosphere as well as an honorable mention in *Time* Magazine for most memorable You Tube moments of 2010. He was compared by one person to the classic Chris Farley character-- Motivational Speaker Matt Foley. Except in the case of Matt Foley, we were laughing with him, and in the case of Phil, we are laughing at him.

I don't know if Phil is intelligent or has great ideas. And let's be honest here--once someone has shown themselves to be borderline crazy by way of a public presentation, there is no going back. You will be labeled, and people aren't known for giving second chances--just ask Howard Dean.

Phil's story is an extreme instance of how the lack of articulation can derail one's career goals, but this same thing happens every day as important decisions get made about who to hire, who to work with, or who to give the contract to. People are swayed by how articulate we are or are not. People make inferences about us based on our ability to present our ideas. In case you were wondering, Mr. Davison was not elected to political office. Go figure.

At this point you may be thinking, "Libby, I am not running for political office....ever." I 100% understand. But don't think that great presentation skills are important only for those with political aspirations. Being articulate matters, no matter the industry you work in. *Inc. Magazine* illuminates this point in a recent article. Staff writer, Marla Tabaka, introduces the reader to Christine Cunneen, CEO of Hire Image, a provider of background employment screenings. Cunneen takes public speaking seriously because it gets her new clients.

Cunneen attests:

> I plant the seeds that will help my business grow. Although we have added numerous clients because of my speaking engagements, many do not happen right away. We added a large university a year after they heard me speak at a conference, and six months later it referred us to another large client," she says. "Another example is the employment attorney who attended one of my speaking engagements and now refers me to

attorneys who post questions on a discussion forum he belongs to. (*Inc Magazine*)

You do not have to be the CEO of your company to yield influence through a great presentation. No matter your location on the company hierarchy, the ability to command an audience with a well-crafted message can separate you from everyone else. *Business Week* magazine measures the power of networking with a term called the influ-tron. In a recent blog post from their site, they write, "A well-publicized speaking gig in front of an appropriate audience has to be worth several thousand influ-trons."

We are living in the age of influence and information. The more people you can "get in front of" at one time and share your niche of expertise with a powerful presentation, the more likely you are to capture market share.

Not convinced? Well here are a few more ideas to solidify the importance of great presentation skills:

1. When making decisions about promotions and leadership roles, many decision makers will consider the ability to craft a great message and deliver it in making their decision. I have worked with decision makers across industries and this is consistently an area of concern.

2. Decision makers in organizations are asking themselves, "Do I trust this person to represent the company inside and outside the office?" That's where presentations become your social proof that you can indeed represent the best interests of the company.

3. Audiences find great public speakers to be smarter than those who are not great at it. This only makes sense. When you are able to articulate your ideas, thoughts, and opinions effectively, people can understand you and connect to you. In turn they will see you as more competent.

4. It is much easier to reach a group of 100 with a knock-their-socks-off presentation than to try and get in front of those 100 people one at a time. It is simple math. If you are in the business of sales this fact can rock your world.

5. We live in a marketplace where the smallest edge can make the difference. More and more people are looking to work with businesses and organizations that are seen as the thought leaders in their respective industry. How do you establish yourself as a thought leader? By doing a great presentation and sharing your expertise.

My own Be a Presentation Super Hero story started a lot earlier than most people's. When I entered high school, I signed up for speech class, and within the first week, I joined the speech and debate team. When I look back on decisions made in this period of my life, it is hands down the second best decision I made (The first was falling in love with a certain fella named Mark Spears, who was also on the speech and debate team and would later become my husband) to line myself up for future success.

In the short term, my participation on the speech and debate team prepared me for college in a way that nothing else offered in high school could. I learned how to use a real research library. I learned critical thinking skills that allowed me to truly engage in the college classroom when challenging ideas came my way, and I learned how to design a presentation for maximum impact.

Quite simply, I learned to Be a Presentation Super Hero.

Would I have been so articulate had I not been in speech and debate? I don't think I would have. Up to that point in my life, I was certainly talkative and I loved to get up in front of people, but articulate? No.

Through sustained and ongoing practice and commitment I LEARNED techniques to shape and mold my message for my audience in such a way that it produced the results I hoped for. In high school it translated into taking home a lot of trophies and even better, my accumulated honors ended with a four-year scholarship that paid for college.

In the long term, those trophies turned into opportunities to "get in front of" some amazing people, clients, groups, and organizations. After years of working on my own presentation skills and doing hundreds of presentations, working with students on how to design and deliver a great presentation, and giving professionals the tools they need to "close the deal" with a presentation, I know this to be true: If you are the person that avoids speaking in public, it will impact your professional trajectory negatively.

If you are the person that avoids speaking in public **it WILL impact your SUCCESS trajectory.**

As you move up the corporate pecking order, you will be required to get in front of the client more and more. Positions of leadership require that you can lead a team of people, recruit the best talent, keep current clients, and bring in new clients. And how do you do that? By communicating. By articulating. By stepping up and being a Presentation Super Hero.

One of the examples I use in my workshops to drive this important point home is to ask my audience, "What if a presentation stood between you and twenty-million dollars?" This is a very real question for many organizations. There is NO industry that does not live or die by it's ability to communicate who they are both inside their organization and outside to their customers and clients. None. Name it. Name one. It is easy to think that there are professions where the ability to articulate is less important. Take the architect for example.

Bravo cc was born when a dear friend called me up from her office and yelled, "Help us!" She was the marketing director for an architecture firm at the time and the principals in her firm needed a public speaking intervention. Like most architecture firms, their win business through a process where they submit a proposal, get short-listed, and interview with decision makers doing a presentation. My new client did a bang up job getting short-listed and into the room to do their presentation. They were failing though to close the deal. The problem? Their presentations were not a stand out from their competition. They were creating and delivering presentations that they thought were great, but their audience did not respond the same way they did. Can you identify? I bet you can because I know this happens all the time.

The interview presentation is used across a number of industries, not just for architects. And the truth is this: Many of the people doing these million dollar presentations don't belong there. They are not great speakers. And they don't seem to care, that is until they begin to realize that they are getting their butts beat every time they go in to an interview presentation.

I feel confident I have made my point thus far on the power of being a Presentation Super Hero. Presentations can be game changers for you and for your organization. Why is it then that so many people struggle with articulating their message to close the deal, land the new client, and win the project? The answer is simple: Today's business presentations suck. I wish there was a better word, but the standard is a low one. Very few professionals and organizations understand the anatomy of a presentation, choose the right people to do the presentation, and invest the time to plan, prepare, and practice a winning presentation. The following list is my own that I think helps to explain the sad state of today's business presentation.

#1: The Abuse of PowerPoint

Today's business presentation is more about the PowerPoint and less about the actual speaker. This formula makes for some abysmal presentations. PowerPoint is not the problem though; it is the people using PowerPoint. They approach this piece of software as a giant notecard. Slides with lines and lines of text, bad and unnecessary graphs, and awful clip art or cheesy and cliched stock photos all come together to create another forgettable presentation. Just Google "Bad Power Point" and you will get pages and pages of articles and examples of this misused piece of software.

Power Point is a back up dancer. YOU are Tina Turner.

For all future presentations remember this simple piece of advise: PowerPoint is a back up dancer. YOU are Tina Turner. No one pays $500 a ticket to go see Tina's back up dancer shake their tail feathers to Proud Mary. They paid to see Tina. YOU are Tina. Your slides are the back up dancer--simply there to make you look good (and when a back up dancer forgets it's place, you get a train wreck called Kevin Federline).

#2: A Packaged, Stale Message

If your marketing department is responsible for creating your presentation, and you have no role in the creation, then shame on you. Why is it that so many organizations believe that marketing people are the only ones with creative ideas? They aren't. You have ideas too. And you should have a hand in YOUR presentation. I am not hating on marketing departments. I am hating on the formula used by so many organizations where the people giving the presentation are not a part of the process. GREAT presentations need collaboration. Creativity, innovation, and new ideas rarely happen in isolation. They happen in the company of other brains/hearts/humans.

For your next presentation, kick the template to the curb and invest the time to create a original presentation. Can I get an AMEN!

#3: Too long

In our hurry up, multi tasked, Angry Birds playing culture, time is money. If you have 45 minutes to do a presentation take only 35 minutes. Your audience will appreciate you for it. Now, in order to do this you must tackle the next issue.

#4: Data Dumps

So many presentations make the mistake of trying to tell the audience everything they have ever known in the history of ever. I call it verbal throw-up. Quit it! If you take the time to get to know your audience, you will be able to identify what they need to know, and you can edit out the other stuff and fluff. Everything is not important.

A fantastic example of information overload is describing in-depth processes or steps for completion of the project as a part of the content of a sales presentation. If you have twenty process slides in your presentation for example, take them out! No one really cares about the process you use, they just want to know--will you do the job I hired you to do, do I trust and like you, and will you stay within the budget? You can't connect to people with process slides. Get rid of them! (The same goes for organizational charts by the way).

#5: Lacks Humanity

Your presentation needs to show that you are three dimensional. The first presentation to a potential client is like a first date. If you use that as your guiding metaphor, it will allow you to connect on an emotional level. We are swayed by people's personality. I want to hear your story. I want to know you and know that you are real. Statistics, facts, and figures are not why people make decisions. They may TELL you that is how they make their decisions, but it is a smokescreen used to justify emotional decision making . We work with people we like. Your presentation should establish that you are more than just credible and qualified to complete the job. It needs to demonstrate that you are also likable.

A few years back, I had an architecture firm on my top ten list of firms I wanted to work with. I had courted them for a while and was waiting for my opportunity to get my foot in the door. One afternoon I got a call from their marketing director asking me if I could come by the next morning and prepare them for a BIG interview that afternoon.

So I had four hours?

"Yes," she replied.

"I'll be there," I told her.

This presentation was a team effort and spearheaded by "Brad". Brad's doppelganger is Peter Fonda (to give you a mental picture) and upon meeting him, I instantly liked him. He has a very gentle and kind demeanor and there was NO ego at work, and I appreciated that a great deal. As we waited for the rest of the team to assemble I went through the slides that had been created and asked some questions. Here is the scenario we were working with:

The presentation was 15 minutes long.

They were the third of four presentations that day.

There were five planned speakers.

The slide deck had 60+ slides in it.

The answer to my next question left me with a lump in my throat and sweat on my brow.

"How much is this contract for?" I asked, fearing the answer.

"Twenty-Seven Million Dollars," he answered without any sign of emotion.

"@#$&*," I thought inside my head.

Over the next four hours, we took potential epic fail of a presentation and created a presentation that included:

TWO speakers + FIFTEEN slides + a smart and interesting metaphor to carry the presentation from start to finish.

As we finished up our presentation bootcamp, Brad told me in a very matter of fact tone, "You know out of the four firms interviewing for this job, we have it on good authority that if the decision were made right now we would come in fourth place."

Fourth place doesn't even get a medal at the Olympics!

I left their office and drove home. I am sure it goes without saying that I was sick to my stomach waiting for the decision. My Lizard brain was in overdrive, to say the least. The next day I received an email from Brad. He had forwarded me the email from the client naming his firm as the top choice, and they would be awarded the contract!

I am certain their presentation is what moved them from fourth place into first place. They did not win a gold medal. They won a TWENTY SEVEN MILLION DOLLAR CONTRACT. Never underestimate the power of a beautiful presentation. But it takes work. Hard work.

To appreciate the idea of a beautiful presentation know this: Passion and Conviction trump Perfection EVERY time. In the context of Be a Presentation Super Hero, what does that mean? It means that if you will stop concentrating your gaze on the perfect and instead remember that those who share their passion and conviction (appropriately of course), are far more enjoyable, persuasive, and effective in their efforts.

Passion and Conviction trump Perfection EVERY time.

I have made my case for the sad state of today's bad business presentation. The challenge lies in re-designing, re-thinking, and re-conceptualizing the presentation into something that looks like nothing you have seen before.

The project to Be a Presentation Super Hero must start somewhere, and I suggest becoming a student of the presentation first before you move on to creating your next presentation. The following is a step-by-step process that I challenge you to use in your journey. These steps are a modification on the activities used in finding your Plan Be. This project can be done as a solo project, or you can use it with your team to challenge everyone to take their presentation skills from mediocre to masterful.

We begin by forging a new relationship.

STEP ONE: Your Three Words + Meet TED.

Becoming a Presentation Super Hero requires you to fully understand your presentation profile. What kind of speaker are you (Or what kind of speaker do you want to be?) We will come back to this idea in a moment, but first I want to inspire you with an introduction to TED.

TED stands for Technology, Entertainment, Design and began in 1984, with industry leaders in these three areas coming together to share short presentations on their areas of expertise. Over time, these TED talks expanded their reach to every conceivable profession and today is regarded as the TOP speaking gig around. Speaking at a TED conference for someone like me is the equivalent of a stage actor getting a gig on Broadway.

TED's motto is, "Ideas Worth Spreading," and that is something I can get behind. Intrigued? You can learn more about the TED movement at www.ted.com.

In almost every topic I teach, I reference a related TED presentation, and I tell my audience to put on their "homework list" a few TED presentations to go back and watch after our workshop.

Becoming a Presentation Super Hero means that you first begin to understand what GREAT presentations look like. How does it walk, talk, feel, and what things make it effective? By identifying the characteristics of a great presentation you will begin to understand how you can become a better presenter.

I created this list around **TEN BIG IDEAS** that will get you started understanding what a stand out presentation looks like.

CHARACTERISTIC	WATCH	LOOK FOR
TELL STORIES	Benjamin Zander The Transformative Power of Classical Music	Note the stories Zander tells throughout the presentation. He takes you through a host of emotions from beginning to end.
BUILD YOUR CREDIBILITY	Sir Ken Robinson Schools Kill Creativity	Sir Robinson does an excellent job of establishing his expertise in his field + making himself credible as a father and someone who cares about kids.
DO SOMETHING UNEXPECTED	Mike Rowe Learning from Dirty Jobs	Rowe tells a visually interesting story in the presentation that catches people off guard a little bit....

CHARACTERISTIC	WATCH	LOOK FOR
HUMANIZE YOURSELF	Jill Bolte Taylor Stoke of Insight	Brain Scientist is IMPRESSIVE on it's own but what happens when Taylor suffers a major stroke and becomes the patient? This story will mesmerize you from beginning to end.
USE EVIDENCE WISELY	Hans Rosling HIV: New Facts and Stunning Visuals	How you present data, evidence, facts, figures, and statistics matters. Learn from one of the pros.
LAUGH AT YOURSELF	Jamie Oliver Teach Every Child about Food	Oliver has a great time speaking to his audience and makes it clear he doesn't miss the irony of an Englishman "lecturing" Americans on the subject matter.
REVEAL YOUR PASSION	Rita Pierson Every Kid Needs a Champion	Just the cadence of Pierson's presentations is passionate. Her facial expressions add to the quality of the presentation; it is impossible to not be infected by her passion.
FILL A GAP IN KNOWLEDGE	Dan Pink The Surprising Science Behind Motivation	Pink establishes that most people are misinformed on the subject and does a great job of teaching us something we probably didn't know.
CREATE AN EMOTIONAL CONNECTION	Shane Koyczan "To this Day"...for the Bullied and Beautiful	For anyone who has been bullied, pushed around, mocked, or made little. Grab a Kleenex!
MOTIVATE, INSPIRE, ENCOURAGE	Brene Brown The Power of Vulnerability	Storyteller, Researcher, and Inspirational speaker. A rare combination.

I encourage you to watch one presentation each day for TEN DAYS. Find about 25 minutes of time where you are not distracted and give your fullest attention to the video. With each video, **challenge yourself to identify THREE take aways that will inspire your future presentations.**

Think about yourself as a speaker and identify the THREE WORDS that best represent your unique style as a speaker. This isn't hard to do. Think about your friendships and the role you play in those friendships. Think about the roles you play when you are working in a team environment. Your strengths that play out in other areas of your life can benefit you as a speaker as well.

My primary speaking style is demonstrated by these three words:

Storyteller | Comedian | Connector

Storyteller and Comedian are fairly self evident. When I use the word connector what I mean is that my ability to connect concepts, evidence, data, and statistics to people's lives, experiences, challenges, and situations is a real strength I have. I am certain that the combination of these three words are why I excel as a speaker.

What are your three words that embody who you are as a presenter?

"I am a Presentation Super Hero!" I am:

_____

_____

_____

and that makes my audience want to listen to what I have to say!

STEP TWO: Identify Your NO-NO List

You cannot experience growth without taking the time to recognize where you are right now and what it will take for you to grow. For me, losing weight is the easiest application of this idea. In the past, I have tried to get away with losing weight without stepping on a scale. I tell myself, "I will know I have lost weight when my jeans get loose." That is my Lizard brain playing tricks on me. I know that losing weight requires that I know where I am starting from so I can chart my progress, so I begrudgingly get on the scale. Yes, I hate it, but I know that if I want to get to where I am going, I will have to account for where I began. That means building your NO-NO list of the things you are going to STOP doing AND then going one step further and replacing the NOs with a YES! action item.

Here is a sample list to inspire you:

NO-NO List	YES!
Avoid Doing a Presentation.	Volunteer to give a presentation. Career Day Presentation Industry Conference Client Education
Wait till the last minute to prepare the presentation.	Schedule Time to Plan, Prepare, & Practice my presentation.
Rely on PowerPoint to Be the Presentation.	Create the Content First and then do the Slides. Consider NOT using slides at all! (shocking!) Rehearse using my slides and get feedback.
Rely on data, statistics and evidence	Use story to connect to the audience.

The YES! List

Here are a few ways to think more about the YES! list from above.

VOLUNTEER

Yes I know. This one may fly in the face of what your past behavior has looked like, but the next time a presentation opportunity comes along, volunteer to do it. It takes a great deal of courage to throw up your hand and say, "I will do the presentation!" but do it anyway. There comes a point where you have a choice: let your fear rule over you like an nobleman would a peasant or tell your fear to suck it. I pick tell my fear to suck it (sorry mom). I hope you will too!

No you don't have to volunteer for presentations that could make or break your success trajectory or that of your organization, but you can start with smaller, less Earth-shattering presentation opportunities. No one runs a marathon without practicing and training first. And training begins with shorter runs. Use this formula for yourself, and start doing some presentations.

Here are a few ideas for volunteering.

1. GIVE A CAREER DAY PRESENTATION:

A Career Day Presentation is a great place to start because in the grand scheme of things an audience of 4th graders, 9th graders, 12th graders, or even a college classroom filled with excited students who want to do what you do, won't make or break your career. Don't think that I mean you should not take this audience seriously. You must! They are a unique group. What appeals to a classroom of 4th graders about what you do will be different from what a classroom of college seniors who want to get a job in your field want to know from you.

A few years ago, I had the opportunity to develop a leadership program for a group of up-and-coming team members for one of my clients. One of the assignments for these future leaders was to present a career-day presentation to me for evaluation and feedback.

The timing for one of the participants could not have been any better because he was presenting to his son's fifth grade class that very afternoon. A real practice session! This always gets my heart beating fast. "Jack" began the presentation, and a few minutes in I realized that Jack had zero idea about how to appeal to a classroom of young people.

One of the things I remember vividly was a slide in his presentation that listed all the architecture degree programs at Texas Universities. This could have been a great point in his presentation had he said, "Look here--if you want to be an architect you don't even have to go too far from home. Within Texas there are a multitude of amazing and well-respected architecture programs that apply to."

Instead he said, "These are all highly competitive degree programs and unless your math and science grades are the top of your class, you won't get in." Seriously? Wow! Talk about the best way to diminish a small flicker of interest in the mind's eye of a young girl or boy who might be the world's next great architect, but isn't the strongest kid in math and science. But Jack didn't understand his audience.

Contrast that with another participant who we will call "Lisa". On the day of her practice Career Day Presentation, she came in carrying a big Ziploc bag containing construction paper, a ruler, a pencil, and other interesting items.

Before she began, she told me, "My career-day presentation is to a 4th grade Girl Scout troop," and she got started. Not only had she prepared a fun activity where each Girl Scout would design their fantasy school, she walked us through the process of how you design a school, what questions you have to ask, what limitations you must work with, and how to create a space that encourages learning. Brilliant!

At the end of the presentation, she passed out a guide to great architecture in Fort Worth, Texas, and told me to grab my mom and dad and make a day seeing the city and the amazing architecture that is all around us.

Lisa knew and understood her audience. It is a presentation I will never forget.

2. SPEAK AT AN INDUSTRY CONFERENCE:

In today's business culture, it is imperative that we set ourselves apart as thought leaders in our industry. What better way to do that than with a conference presentation? If you participate in industry organizations, apply to speak at their annual conference. Develop an area of expertise, and share it at every conference you attend.

The cumulative effect is that over time people will come to see you as a content expert. Speaking at a conference filled with your peers or clients can be intimidating. If you take the time to develop a dynamic, energetic, and relevant presentation, a great deal of the fear and loathing will diminish. The smart cookies at Ethos3 hit the nail on the head in a recent blog post. They write:

> If you can deliver a sensational performance to boot, you can expect even greater returns on the investment of time and effort. The fact of the matter is that in our current economic client, companies are increasingly valuing employees who demonstrate a willingness to go above and beyond their job descriptions. In the past, such overt efforts may have been misconstrued as selfish or even mutinous; today, most companies don't want any employee whose ambitions are limited to the scope of their current job and business hours.

> So if you want to build a platform, start identifying opportunities to present. Where possible, seek opportunities that create a win-win situation for yourself and your company. Working together, you'll both go far. (www.ethos3.com)

If your organization attends an industry conference every year and is not represented with at least one presenter then shame, shame, and shame again. Conferences are a critical place for dispensing your expertise. Take the time to find out when speaker submissions are due for the next conference and submit to speak. Tell yourself, "I will rock their face off!" and you will.

You may not be selected to speak the first time you submit, but don't let that discourage you. Keep trying. Sometimes you have to achieve a particular speaker rating at a regional/state conference before you will "qualify" to speak a a nation/international conference. If the national or international conference doesn't choose you, look to regional or state conferences as the first step in the right direction. It takes time to establish yourself as a speaking powerhouse, but if you are committed it will happen.

3. EDUCATE YOUR CLIENTS:

One of the services you can (and should) provide your client is education tied to your industry. Every industry evolves and changes, and you have the opportunity to be the organization that keeps your client up-to-date on these changes. Every quarter, schedule an hour session with your clients and those people you want to be your client to come and do a mini-workshop or learning session. Once they are there, you have their undivided attention and can educate them on changes in your industry that they need to be aware of. That, in my estimation, is a great example of what we call a value add. You can bring donuts and coffee or sandwiches and chips to attract attendees and voila, you are now giving a captivating presentation. (The youth pastor at my church was smart. He knew that if we wanted to get visitors to attend our youth group that donuts would be a big draw. He would tell us "Tell your friends we have donuts." NEVER underestimate the power of the donut.)

I have had the privilege of working with a number of architecture firms over the last five years. Of all the firms whose work resonated with me the most, VLK architects in Fort Worth, Texas wins this distinction. VLK designs smart and modern schools. At my very core I am an educator, so the chance to learn how architecture and design impacts learning was obviously a draw. My work with them has taught me how to "speak architect," and I have so many fond memories of working with their team.

The evolution of the school over the last one hundred years fascinates me. When I go home to Lubbock, Texas, and see my elementary school (which is just across the street from my childhood home), I am dumbstruck at how it compares to today's elementary school. Why have schools changed? Because over time, through research and inquiry, it has been established that the environment in which a student is placed impacts her learning. This knowledge informs the way VLK designs each and every school.

If we take that very simple idea and apply it to client education as a presentation opportunity, why not bring that knowledge and understanding to existing clients and future clients? Through the vehicle of a great presentation you can do just that.

Stop for a moment and consider your industry. How can you define your expertise? My husband works for HP and has been in this industry for most of his career. When Mark was a fresh-faced, twenty-two year old, the copier industry was well...the copier industry. The evolution of his field over the last eighteen years is incredible. The explosion of technology has transformed the world of the copier into something far more exciting and interesting than what it was when he started.

My husband is incredibly knowledgable about his field, and I am always baffled by his understanding of the complexities around the products he sells. Lucky for him, he is also a great public speaker, and his position in his organization gives him many opportunities to share his knowledge. I am certain beyond a shadow of a doubt that much of his career success can be attributed to his ability to share this knowledge anytime, anywhere, anyplace, and to any audience.

Do you currently set yourself apart as a thought leader in your industry?

Do you have a specialized area of knowledge or a niche that you could share with people and they would be better for having listened?

How often do you put yourself in front of your client and future client to educate them?

If the answer is "never" then you are in a position to change that today.

PLAN I PREPARE I PRACTICE

Far too many presentations are put off until the last minute. Have you ever said, "I'm just going to wing it?" Not a great strategy. I have seen many a professional crash and burn because they convinced themselves that they are going to, "Just get out there and talk," and it will magically work out. Please understand this: The BEST public speakers work hard at their craft. They have spent years perfecting their presentation style and eventually reach a place where it looks natural. But that is the rub, it LOOKS natural. Seasoned speakers are calm, comfortable, and conversational with an audience because they have worked at it diligently.

If you will schedule the time to plan, prepare, and practice every presentation you give, you will be that much closer to realizing the goal of becoming a Presentation Super Hero. Where do you begin? Good question.

Your perfect starting point is to implement a process that will walk you through all the required steps to create a presentation that your audience will not soon forget. The following are my suggestions for you to use in any presentation you give. Tweak them as you see fit, and refine the process to suit you perfectly. Know this: This process does not work if you don't use it.

Once you have chosen your topic, use these steps to craft your presentation. For a 60 minute presentation I estimate the time you will spend on each step.

PLAN I PREPARE I PRACTICE I PRESENT	TIME
1. Audience Analysis. EVERY presentation should begin here. Unfortunately, far too many people do not spend the time being thoughtful about who their audience is. Ask yourself these questions: *What does my audience lay in bed at night and hope for, dream about, worry about? How can I help them with one or more of these issues? *What does my audience know about me, my industry, my topic? What "gap in knowledge" can I fill for them that will make them smarter, faster, more successful? *What do I have in common with my audience? *Will my audience be sympathetic, apathetic, neutral, or hostile to me and/or my topic?	60 to 90 Minutes

PLAN | PREPARE | PRACTICE | PRESENT	TIME
2. My Credibility. Establish your expertise on the topic. Establish your organization's credibility. Establish your credibility as a HUMAN BEING. Yes, you may have content expertise but that is not enough.	60 minutes
3. Generate Content ✶What THREE BIG things do I want my audience to take away from my presentation? ✶What gap in knowledge can I fill? ✶What do I want my audience to DO after they hear my presentation?	60 to 90 minutes
4. Research Your own expertise is important, but you need to build your presentation on reliable data, evidence, facts, and statistics. For each of the THREE BIG IDEAS you will cover in your presentation, look for one to three (Depending on the length of your presentation) to illuminate each idea. Consider other experts, research studies, client testimonials, books, articles, etc.	3 to 4 hours
5. Add Stories You have THREE BIG IDEAS you will cover in your presentation. Now, find a story for each of these three ideas that you can use in the presentation. They can be personal stories or stories you heard about, read about, etc.	60 to 90 minutes
6. Get Visual The power of PowerPoint is the visual impact it can have on a presentation. Before you start creating slides, ask yourself this: Do I need a PowerPoint? You might just do something amazing with out a PowerPoint. If you decide you need slides then remember: ✶No bullet points. ✶Keep slides to one idea per slide ✶Use striking and interesting visuals. No cheesy clip art or cliched stock photography.	3 to 4 hours

PLAN I PREPARE I PRACTICE I PRESENT	TIME
7. Practice time Speaking the presentation out loud in your car does not constitute practice. Instead, use the following: ✳Speak out loud from beginning to end two to three times by yourself. Edit as needed. ✳Find three or four warm bodies who can give you feedback (more on feedback later) and critique your delivery style, your content, your slides. Run through the presentation one time. Edit. ✳The day of the presentation, deliver the presentation one time all the way through and find someone to sit in and listen.	2 to 3 hours
8. Go kick ass	60 minute presentation
Total Time Invested	12 to 15 hours

SEEK FEEDBACK

When a company launches a new product, they don't just put it out there and see if it sticks--they test it first. I love, love, love an episode from *Mad Men* (one of the best TV shows of the past five years), where a cosmetic company hires Sterling Cooper Advertising Agency to help them grow their market share of the cosmetics industry.

They gather up all the secretaries in the agency (The show takes place in the 1960's when there were no female ad executives. Imagine!), and put them in a room to test their products and see what kind of feedback they get.

The episode is fascinating but the message for our uses is this: ask YOUR AUDIENCE before you move forward. If you are going to embrace becoming more articulate, one of the best things you can do for yourself is to get an audience who will tell you what you do well and where you need some polishing. And take this seriously, because it is serious.

When you seek feedback from another person, you have to be VERY specific about what kind of feedback you want and need. There is a tendency among people to say, "Yeah that was really good." This is due in part to the fact that we don't typically deconstruct a presentation and look at all it's various sides, layers, and angles. The other reason is because you are most likely to ask people you like and know well, and these people may not feel comfortable giving you candid feedback.

With that being said, what will you ask them to look for in your presentation? Here are some direct and specific questions to give your evaluator to give you feedback.

1. Structure--does the presentation flow well? Are the main ideas in the right order to produce maximum impact?
2. Are there appropriate emotional appeals in the presentation? What did you FEEL during the presentation? NAME the emotions (happy, entertained, sad, curious, fearful, guilty, annoyed, irritated, bored, defensive).
3. Content--is there anything in the presentation that does not aid in helping me build my case? If I had to cut out something what would be the FIRST thing you would get rid of?
4. Likewise, is there anything MISSING from the presentation that I might cover?
5. As you listened to the presentation were there questions you were asking yourself? What are they?
6. Balance--is the balance between story and facts/figures/statistics good?

PUT POWERPOINT IN IT'S PLACE

If there is one easy fix to your next presentation, this is it. PowerPoint is not bad. The people using it are the problem. Becoming a Presentation Super Hero means taking chances and having the courage to do something that no one else is doing. What if, just maybe, this one time you ditched the Power Point?

Think about it: Abraham Lincoln did not need a PowerPoint to move a nation and forever change the course of history. Martin Luther King had a dream and shared it with an audience that hung on his every word, and there was no screen littered with awful clip art of kids of all colors holding hands. Maya Angelou told us she knows why the caged bird sings, and she used the power of language + her powerful voice to do it. No screen, no projector, no clicker, no laser pointer, no bad animation, no slides. Nada. Nothing. These people were the show!

My recommendation is to start small. If you are speaking for 5 to 10 minutes then ditch the power point. You can do it. I swear. Challenge yourself to be the entire presentation, and tap into your abilities to captivate an audience on your own.

There are going to be times that you need to use a PowerPoint. No problem--I understand, as I use slides in about 75% of my presentations. I feel you. The challenge becomes this: How can you create slides that compliment the presentation and makes you look good? Below are my recommendations for the preparation and the presentation of your slides. In the resource section at the end of the book you will also find some inspiration for learning how to put PowerPoint back in it's place.

1. Keep every slide simple. One idea per slide is an ideal goal and that means editing down to the key concept you want to talk about.
2. Get rid of bullet points. The use of bullet points in slides means you are really just creating giant, illuminated notecards.
3. Be visual. The power of any slide is that it can provide a visual reference point for what you are talking about. Use high quality graphics that are interesting and add to the experience of your presentation.
4. Avoid cliche. Too many people design their slides using clip art and cliched images. You want to avoid this as much as possible! Start by looking at other slide presentations that will inspire you and give you great ideas.
5. Be consistent. Start your slides with a top slide that is the "style sheet" for the entire presentation. What fonts will you use (no more than three), what colors are you using for background, headlines, etc? Make sure you consistently apply these rules to every slide in the deck!

*to learn more about designing great slide go to www.slideshare.net/Bravocc

Step Three: Use Story

Stories move us. Stories connect us to the human experience. A well told story has the potential to make us laugh, cry, experience fear, anger, regret, healing, and more. A GREAT story makes us feel multiple things. We want to know each other's story and we want to share our story.

I challenge you for just one day to document how many stories you tell and are told to you in conversation. Time with my friends is about telling stories. I get to be with my two best college girlfriends, Lizzy and Teri, three or four times a year. It is fascinating how much of our time together is centered around telling stories that have been told thousands of times before but each time we love and enjoy the story as if it were the first time we heard it. These stories take on new meaning and contour over the years as we age, mature, and honestly acknowledge the march of time.

What is YOUR story?

If your answer is, "I don't know," you are in trouble. Stories are powerful and persuasive modes of communication and they are one of the ways that people determine if they like you. A good story is a demonstration of who you are versus telling me who you are. My friend Millie has a rule, if someone ever tells you something like, "I am a classy person" then what they have really told you is they want you to see them as having class, but they have yet show that they do, in fact, have class. But telling a story is a much better vehicle for demonstrating who you truly are--kind, funny, smart, passionate, or classy.

I remember, as a little girl, that every evening my parents would watch the evening news on ABC. At the end of every broadcast, Paul Harvey would come on and do, "And now for the rest of the story." I hated the news, but for some reason I actually enjoyed Mr. Harvey. That tag line, "And now for the rest of the story," has always stayed with me, and I use it in many of my workshops to illustrate the power of story.

For me, "The rest of the story," is what does not get said in the story, but on some level is understood by the listener. Allow me to explain.

Every great story has an implied meaning behind it. You don't have to say, "See what this story means is that we value our people here at XYZ corporation." The story conveys the message and it does it so much more beautifully and convincingly than a chart, graph, power point slide, fact, figure, or statistic ever could.

One of the greatest failures I see in business presentations is the use of facts, figures, and statistics in favor of storytelling. This is understandable on some level-- after all, it is business, and data and evidence would seem to carry a great deal of weight in decision making. Likewise, when asked, most people would tell you they make their decisions based on the facts. But they don't. Don't believe them. We all want to believe that our decisions come down to the raw data, that there is no emotion involved, but there is. There always is an emotional component at work. Even in cases of government contracts, where a sophisticated rubric has been developed to try and overcome human emotion in the decision making process, emotion still plays a role.

Please don't misunderstand me--I am not suggesting that data and evidence have no role in decision making. Both do, and both are important. I am not offering an either/or scenario. My advice is that you have a healthy balance between the evidence and storytelling. Let them work together. When I work with a group to become better presenters I tell them, "Story is what gives your data and evidence wings and let's it fly."

The two should work together to build your case, whatever your case may be.

Paul Smith, author of *Lead with a Story: A Guide to Crafting Business Narratives that Captivate, Convince, and Inspire*, illuminates my point. He shares in an interview with Forbes Magazine:

> Storytelling is useful when heavy influence is required like leading change, or making recommendations to the boss. But it's also good for delicate issues like managing diversity and inclusion, or giving people coaching and feedback in a way that will be received as a welcome gift. It can help bring out more of people's creativity, or help them rekindle the passion for their work.

A few years ago I worked on a project for a non-profit organization. They wanted to create a speaker's bureau and equip those who had championed their cause with a presentation they could share in their community to find new donors.

When I first began working with the group, what I found was a pile of old presentations that followed the formula of most every business presentation I had seen to date: Too many slides, too much information, and too much data. There were charts and graphs in eighteen point font that could not be seen on a screen by anyone sitting more than say, ten inches from the screen. This was not a new scenario for me. I had seen it too many times.

In our training workshop with the new recruits, I placed a heavy emphasis on the role of telling the story around the project, telling their own story as it relates to the project, and to weave these throughout the presentation.

When we reassembled to practice the new presentation, our first volunteer came up, and began by telling a story about being raised in Suburban Chicago in the 1960's, in a middle class family that was very average, and did average things. His exposure to the arts (the mission of this group), was limited to say the least.

He got married, and like any good husband who wants to keep his new wife happy, he obliged her when she wanted to see CATS!, a popular Broadway musical. The experience he had was most certainly not what he expected. He was captivated, energized, and he wanted to see more.

This story played a role throughout his presentation as he referenced back to it at key moments. In the end of his presentation, he hit on the importance of arts education for students and he asked us to remember his childhood and his lack of arts education.

In a word, his presentation was lovely. Beyond lovely, he struck a chord in all of us as he invited us to experience this awakening that he felt as a grown man experiencing the arts for the first time in his life. This story allowed us the opportunity to also reflect on our own interactions with the arts, and remember how it felt when we learned that we also love the arts.

When he was finished, we did a quick go round the table to provide him with a critique. We started with what we liked, and as expected everyone commented on the power of his story. When he returned to his seat I said, "The best part of your presentation, and the most convincing part was your story. It persuaded me in a way no chart, graph, or piece of data could have."

He replied, "I have you to thank for that. It would have never occurred to me tell that story."

Wow.

Now is the time to learn to use story in your presentations.

Do you know a masterful storyteller? If so, start to pay attention to their style. You will probably notice that their storytelling creates moments of drama and suspense, and they use their entire being to tell the story. Everything he or she does moves the story forward. This includes their voice, their language choices, the use of their body, their facial expressions, and their timing. They pause, they speed up, their voice gets louder and more animated. All these things work together as a package to allow you, the listener, to see, feel, and hear the story. Do not for a moment believe that this is just natural to them. Much like public speaking is the combination of art + science, so too is storytelling. The BEST storytellers take this communication tool seriously, and they have invest the time and effort to become great at it.

If you do not, in fact, know a great storyteller then let me give you a few resources of my own. Earlier, I introduced you to TED. One of the videos I recommended was Benjamin Zander's, conductor of the Boston Philharmonic, presentation on classical music.

Zander's presentation about classical music (Which on it's face does not seem a very interesting or compelling topic to the average bear, including myself!), is delightful and every time I have watched it, I feel joy. He begins his presentation with a fun and light-hearted story to set the tone for the audience.

From there, Zander begins to weave a story about how a young person fares when taking piano lessons and the progress and evolution of the piano player. There is a character--the piano student, there is fun and humor as Zander tells us what it is like to learn the piano, and I suspect the laughter is due in part to the fact that many of us are in fact failed piano students (myself included).

Next, he shares a story about someone he spoke to at another presentation,and the theory of the "one butted" piano player is revealed. At this point, Zander has moved into the audience and literally touches someone in the audience to SHOW us what he did to the young man in the story. Zander's arms are flying and he gesticulates wildly. The reaction of his audience is testimony enough that they are loving him, and by loving him they are more likely to consider his sales pitch. Because Zander is selling. He is selling the idea that classical music is worthy of our attention (and remember too WE ARE ALL IN SALES!).

In the conclusion of his presentation, Zander tells a story of a woman who was sent to Auschwitz with her brother. The tone and feel of Zander's presentation takes a turn. We have had a wonderful time up to this point, and have laughed a number of times, but there is something fundamentally important that Zander wants everyone to take away. There is power and possibility for healing that can come from classical music. This story demonstrates this simple truth. Bravo.

It is worth noting here, as you challenge yourself to become a better communicator, that Zander begins and ends his presentation with a STORY. Tuck that away for yourself the next time you are called to speak to a group.

All in all, this twenty minute presentation FEELS like a story from beginning to end doesn't it? There are NO slides (Oh my! revolutionary!), no charts or graphs, no hard core data, but instead Zander makes his case through compelling appeals to his audience to experience classical music. He injects humor throughout, and dispels the notion that those who love classical music are stuck up, elite, and one dimensional.

You will find that the most popular talks at a TED gathering use story to move the audience. These speakers understand the POWER of Story. Story persuades us. Story moves us. Story transforms us.

Before we move forward, I have one last observation. In our hurry up, get to the next thing on our schedule kind of world, do you think anyone in the audience with Zander that day pulled out their cell phone and checked their email, text messages, or updated their Facebook status about what they had for lunch? I doubt that one person there did. They were captivated. Zander created what my friend Micah refers to as a "no phone zone," where, for a few minutes, that group took part in a shared moment together where nothing else mattered. Those moments and experiences are rare in our culture, and when they come along we feel lucky to have been there.

I have yet to see data, evidence, charts, graphs, facts, figures, or statistics do that. In fact the opposite happens. We get bored and overwhelmed by too much evidence, and when we feel that way, we check out and doodle on our paper, pull out our phone, and check out mentally.

As you begin to take storytelling in your presentations more seriously, you will take more time to gather great stories for future use. Over the years I have encouraged my own clients to create their own storytelling folder. This folder includes not only their own stories but great stories that cross their path that could be used at a later time. *"The Story Factor,"* by Annette Simmons, is the best book written on storytelling. It is a rich collection of stories from her experiences, her clients, fables, myths, and legends from history. I can't imagine the time it took her to assemble all these stories in the pages of her excellent book, but I highly recommend you read it if you want to take storytelling seriously as a part of your own Plan Be.

Your story folder can be a real folder where you jot notes and gather articles, or it can be an electronic folder on your desktop where you keep your stories. I do both. When something interesting or captivating crosses my path, I want to remember it and keep it for future reference. You never know when a story may be perfect for your next presentation.

Now you have a better understanding of how to become a Presentation Super Hero. As you can see, like anything worth doing, it takes focus, persistence, and a great deal of courage to tackle an area that may not come naturally to you. Will you be "on the circuit" speaking to groups of all sizes? Maybe. You never know. There may be a great speaker living in you just waiting to be unleashed.

You must truly believe in the power of a presentation and the impact it can have on those who hear your presentation if you want to Be a Presentation Super Hero. No matter where you are in the journey, I hope this chapter gave you the tools you need to get started.

BLOG EXTRA!
You gotta start em' early

My daughter is running for student council today at her school. I don't know if she will win the election as the politics in the 5th grade are just brutal! She asked me to help her prepare her speech, and I thought I would share it here to illustrate how I can even apply the principles I teach to a ten year old's speech to her classmates.

Maddie was a little nervous while she was practicing her speech, so I did what I have done for countless other people--I gave her some stage directions. I put them in all capital letters and inside brackets, so she would know not to read that out loud! As she practiced, her biggest challenge was to not read too fast, so I started her notecard with this direction:

NOTECARD #1:
(DON'T READ TOO FAST! SLOW)
"Did you know that a survey I read said people are more scared of giving a speech than of death? Seriously? but I want to run for student council and that means giving a speech.... so here I go."

Maddie had three ideas on why people should vote for her. We used this one as the first because it has the smallest impact. I tried to inject a little humor, but who knows with ten-year-olds if they will laugh at my little attempt at humor. Yeah--I could have told her to just burp really loud--kids love that stuff--but I don't believe in pandering.

NOTECARD #2:
(REMEMBER TO MAKE EYE CONTACT)
"First of all I think I will do a GREAT job on the maverick morning news. I love watching the news and I think it would be fun to be the newscaster. Have you seen Katie Couric on the TV news? Well I want to be the fifth grade Katie Couric!"

Now for the last idea. This idea is a direct connection to the posters she made to hang up around the school: "Maddie Spears is Mint," and she put packages of spearmint gum all over the poster. It was pretty cute and apparently a hit because all the kids wanted to know if they could have a piece if they vote for her.

NOTECARD #3
(BREATHE, SMILE)
I also like helping other people and I think student council is a great way to serve our school by helping students and people in our community too.

For her conclusion we really struggled. I had some clever ideas, but Maddie vetoed all of them because they were lame and stupid. Her words. So we settled on something pretty simple.

NOTECARD #4
(MAKE EYE CONTACT WITH EVERYONE)
"The last thing is something I think is a really good idea. Ever wish you could chew gum at school? Well I think we should change twin day to "Double Mint Twin Day". You would still dress like your friend and be twins but the best part? You get to chew gum in school....ALL DAY LONG! I think that would be really cool."

NOTECARD #5
"You probably have some great ideas too for things we could do at our school. If you vote for me I hope you will tell me your great ideas and I will try and make them happen!"

To compliment the speech I made her a T-Shirt that said "Vote for Maddie" on the front and "I want to be your DoubleMint Twin" on the back and did black and green to match her gum packets.

Will she win? Who knows. I am more proud that she can get up in front of a crowd and articulate her ideas. She is a pretty great kid, and if mom and dad could vote she would be a shoe in. Fifth graders are a pretty fickle bunch. But in the end, we had fun working on the posters and speech, and win or lose, she is still a great kid.

BLOG EXTRA!
Jamie Oliver and his Food Revolution

Every day millions of dollars are spent on marketing and advertising, and yet in so many organizations, the power of the presentation is an afterthought. In the last two weeks I have a friend who has been given the task of organizing a group of presentations from people in his company for a convention. The audience for these presentations are their very own clients--an audience that is tenuous at all times. There is no such thing as a customer for life anymore. So one would think that A LOT of time, effort, and expertise would be invested in the creation of quality presentations and presenters.

This has not been the case. It has been the opposite.

High levels of anxiety, frustration, and anger have been felt on the part of the organizer because he has not been given the time or resources to adequately prepare this group. He texted me a few days back and told me I would kill myself if I saw their slides. That is probably a bit of an overstatement, but I got his point.

So let it be said:

YOUR PRESENTATION IS ONE
OF THE MOST IMPORTANT
MARKETING TOOLS AVAILABLE TO YOU.
STOP MESSING IT UP!

If you want to see it done right, take twenty minutes of your day and watch Jamie Oliver's TED presentation on his food revolution. Here is what you will find: It is not highly polished or manipulative at all. It is engaging, funny, serious, and human. Jamie is totally transparent. His audience shows their appreciation with applause and enthusiasm for his message. Jamie engages all our senses, uses technology to HELP the presentation but not become the presentation. All in all, it is not a perfect presentation, and for me that is what actually makes it perfect.

Take Jamie's lead and use his approach in your next presentation. The more three dimensional you can be, the more your audience will respond to your message.

Don't take yourself so seriously that you end up with a stale, pre-packaged, one-size-fits-all presentation. That is a formula for failure, and your audience will more than likely check out and do something else (angry birds anyone?) while they count the minutes until you finish.

Can you imagine if more business people like my friend's company took a few risks and didn't do the business as usual presentation? Imagine the impact they would have if they DID NOT do what everyone else does in these conference presentations: Boring slides with bullet point after bullet point, content that does not truly fit the audience, statistics, facts, figures, and evidence that have no context, messages that don't incorporate stories to illuminate their ideas. You know what I am talking about as I am certain you have been held hostage by these kinds of presentations many times.

That's a world I want to live in. I want more Jamie Oliver's in the business world doing presentations. I bet you do too.

BLOG EXTRA!
Shakespeare and the Athlete

I asked Harry Winters to share an great story that he used in a presentation that I worked with him on. The presentation itself was to drum up interest and donations to an Arts project in the Dallas/Ft. Worth area and Harry is one of the core group of people who generously donate their own time helping this project gain momentum.

Here is his story:

For a variety of reasons, when I finished the 9th grade, I decided not to continue playing football in high school. Having grown up in a family where couch "potato-ism" was not allowed, I was required to be involved in something, anything, after school. A very good family friend suggested I give theater a try.

As the son of a salesman, and possessing an outgoing and curious personality, she thought it might be a good fit, which proved to be true. Over the next three years, I proceeded to participate in every production staged at J.J. Pearce and had the time of my life. The highlight of my high school theater career, the "teaching moment" for me and a lot of my friends, came during my junior year.

I was playing, Petruchio, the lead actor in William Shakespeare's "The Taming of the Shrew." The play was presented as part of a statewide drama competition and had been condensed into a half-hour one act play. We did not change any of Shakespeare's text, just concluded the play at the end of Act I, shortly after the comedy's hero and heroine, Kate and Petruchio, meet.

Before the actual competition, we performed the play for our fellow students, who were given a break from their usual English classes to take an on-campus field trip to see our play in the high school theater.

I was a junior at Pearce in 1981 and the Big Man on Campus, both literally and figuratively, was a football player named Ray Childress. As a high school senior, Ray was about 6 ft., 5 inches tall, weighed around 260 lbs. and was very fast. He was a blue chip high school athlete, who went from J.J. Pearce to Texas A&M where he was a two time All-American. In 1985, Ray was drafted with the third pick by the Houston Oilers where he had an outstanding career spanning eleven seasons and was a five-time Pro Bowler. In 2010, he was named to the Texas Sports Hall of Fame.

Back to 1981. I was a goofy, good humored, drama dude walking to lunch with three or four of my friends. Outside the cafeteria, the seniors who ate first, because, well, they were seniors, were hanging out waiting for the bell to ring them to class. As I turned to go inside, I heard a deep voice behind me say, "Hey, Winters, come here..." I turn around and standing head and shoulders above the other football players, assorted friends and pretty girlfriends, I saw Ray gesturing to me. My friends look at me like, "what have you done?" and I look back with an expression that says, "umm, I don't know?"

Now, you have to understand-- people at J.J. Pearce were not afraid of Ray. He didn't take advantage of his immense size and strength and was never a bully. Still, he was an imposing presence and everyone had a great deal of respect for him. So, it was kind of startling to have him call my name. I walked over, looked up and said "Uhh, yeah? What's up, Ray?"

"You were really good in that play, man. I don't like reading Shakespeare in class, but that play was really funny and I liked it. It was cool." Ray's friends, and their very pretty girlfriends looked at us and, as I recall it today, everyone was pretty much smiling and it was a really nice moment. I said, "Thanks, man" and then he went back to talking with his friends and I went on to lunch.

Certain experiences, like plays and music, are meant to be performed. While they might be enjoyed by reading or listening to them alone in one's on room, the power of experiencing a performance can be very strong.

Even in high school, where cliques and social groups can create a fractious environment, a play can build a bridge between two very different groups of people. If a very well respected high school athlete enjoys Shakespeare, or another play, and the arts, he can have a powerful influence on all of the people around him.

Theater and art can have an impact that lasts a lifetime. It can encourage people to pass on a legacy of love of the arts to their children. Ray is happily married to his high school sweetheart, Kara Childress, and they live in Houston and have four terrific kids. I sent an e-mail to Kara asking if it was okay if I used Ray's name in this story. She said that Ray would be happy to help and then related the following:

"We have 4 kids...they have all been active in theatre. They go to The Kinkaid School in Houston, and have a great Theater Arts dept. They are involved in Children's Theater. Wells, our 6'4" son (who will be playing football at Columbia in the fall) was Dopey in Snow White - hysterical that he was one of 7 dwarfs!"

I love Harry's story! The arts is for everyone and his story is the best example of this truth. When I met Harry, I knew instantly that he was a very gifted storyteller and I am sure his years in the theater department helped to shape his storytelling abilities.

No matter the topic or what you need to accomplish, dig deep and find the story that will relate to the audience and show the the power of your message.

BLOG EXTRA!
Storytelling and the Curse of Knowledge

In our lunch, learn, and lead workshop with a client this week we are looking in great depth at how to generate sticky ideas for our presentations. I am hoping to get some feedback leading up to Friday that will help us to wrap our head around the concepts of sticky ideas. One of the most profound, yet simple ideas that comes out of Chip and Dan Heath's book, *Made to Stick,* is "The Curse of Knowledge" heretofore referred to as: CofK. Ok...

The CofK concept is pretty simple in it's description--once we know something, it is hard to imagine what it was like to not know it. Done. I have to remember this when teaching presentation and slide design. I have years of experience doing this--most people don't. So I have to carefully construct my messages to fit the experiences of my audience.

Now, if you have ever had to suffer through the pains of helping your son or daughter with multiplication you can understand CofK at work. As an adult, with years of experience multiplying numbers, we have all learned the little tricks that help us to multiple even the most difficult of numbers. Just the other night I was working with my daughter on 7, 8, and 9. I was hoping the pattern that emerges when multiplying with the number 9 would be obvious. You know it right?

9 18 27 36 45 54 63 72 81 90 99 108 117 126 135 144 153 162 171 180
Do you see the pattern?
You probably do.

The number in the ten's place is going up as we climb to 90 and it is going down in the one's place. When we get to 99, we start over again and the tens place goes up one while the one's place goes down one. But my daughter did not see the pattern on her own. And this made me frustrated. How could she not see it?

Because I am familiar with the CofK, I was quick to remember that I probably didn't figure out the pattern on my own either (I'm no rain man mind you), and it is more likely that an adult pointed it out to me. And with that realization I was able to then modify my instruction to accommodate for the fact that she does not have the same knowledge base as I do.

So, I am wondering--how does the CofK get in the way of your story about you or your organization? Consider for example if you work in a highly specialized industry. Do you tend to take for granted that not everyone knows the same things you know? (Computer People can be among the worst! Sorry but it's true!)

The best stories resonate. They can't do this if you are operating from the belief that everyone knows and understands everything you know and understand.

BLOG EXTRA!
Storytelling + Slides = Love

I was cruising the aisles of the business section at Barnes and Noble yesterday in search of new alluring book titles and came across a book on leadership and presentations that looked interesting. I opened it up to the table of contents and noticed a section on PowerPoint so I turned to the page indicated where I read "how many of you have ever left a presentation and said 'Wow he/she has a great PowerPoint!'? No one right?" The writer went on to suggest that great leaders don't need PowerPoint for a great presentation. That may be true in some cases. But to then make the assumption that no one has ever been moved by a great Power Point? Well, I respectfully disagree.

Slides in a presentation have the ability to create a visual experience that a stand alone speaker could never achieve no matter how amazing her language choices might be. That is just the truth of the matter. I recognize the place of my slides--to provide visual impact to my message--and I design them accordingly. On many occasions my workshop and presentation attendees have commented on how great my slides were and well, I humbly agree. I work HARD at it. Why?

Because SEEING is powerful.

Because the research is conclusive: people are more likely to remember a message when all their senses are employed.

Because audiences want a multi sensory experience.

Because audiences have a shorter attention span and are more likely to zone out without something to look at.

Because Because Because.

Slides are not bad. The people who design them are usually the problem.

If you have never left a presentation and said "Her Power Point rocked" you would certainly know it when one did in fact, well, rock. It would make an impact. You would sit up and take notice.

Slides are not going to go away. People are going to keep using PowerPoint. I for one am glad for it, because it allows me to work with my clients to help them design slides that Rock. I shall not throw the book under the bus because I did not read the whole thing and I suspect there is probably some great advice inside the book. But suggesting that great leaders who are great speakers don't use Power Point or Slides in their presentations is just flat out wrong.

Just ask Steve Jobs.....

BLOG EXTRA!
Story and Trust

My husband Mark should have already headed to the airport to catch his 3:30 flight but me thinks he is delaying his departure so he can watch the Tiger Wood's Press Conference. On the different morning shows today a variety of interested observers tried to guess at what kinds of questions Tiger would have to field at said press conference. Um....that is a stretch. I'll betcha a moon pie and RC cola he gets asked about his katrillion marital indiscretions, his relationship to a seedy, steroid giving Canadian doctor, and all things in-between. And then there will be a question or two about how he can get back to winning.

99% of the questions he will be asked in said press conference will come down to this: CREDIBILITY and CHARACTER (Of which it appears Mr. Woods has very little of.) 1% will be about the actual game of golf (and even those will be asked within the context of his complete lack of moral judgment: "How do you play good golf this week after having been revealed you are a schmuck?")

And therein lies the lesson. It doesn't matter if you bounce a ball, throw a ball, hit a ball with a stick, run a company, make a product that changes lives, represent your community as an elected official, raise kids, teach kids, or scoop ice cream onto a cone--your credibility and character are the most precious things you have and should be managed at every turn (Managed not manipulated--those are different things indeed.)

In the newest issue of SIGolf, Brad Faxon weighs in with "How Woods Can Reclaim His Place in the Game." I imagine Tiger's group of well meaning handlers have asked themselves the same question ad naseum. I envision them at a table throwing out ideas on how to do just that. "How about a televised apology to all the people he has hurt sitting in a row with Tiger behind a lectern talking about how sorry he is?" That won't be awkward or anything. But it was. Know why? Because you can't manufacture this stuff. Just putting a camera on an apology makes us ALL question your sincerity.

What I found far more interesting in this issue of SIGolf was not Brad Faxon's piece but the ad on the inside cover of the magazine from Titleist (you know the other golf ball maker, not Nike--the maker of Tiger's preferred golf ball). I googled the ad to see if anyone had caught the subtle stab at Tiger but found nothing.

The ad features a gaggle of professional players and why they "trust" the Titleist ball. The add reads "Stories of Trust at Augusta" (ouch!)
I think a clever team of marketing people who are smart, savvy, and just knew that the underlying message is: Trust = Character which = Credibility = Not Tiger Woods = We are so stinkin' smart because he doesn't use our golf ball. Maybe I am wrong. Maybe I am reading too deep into this one or maybe I am not. I think Titleist knows

how important credibility and character are even for guys who hit a little ball for a living. I think they know other people know it too.

At the end of the day every person will make their own call on whether they will let Tiger back into their good graces and even go so far as to root for him when he is on the green. For me, I won't. As a fan I am done with the man. I don't care if he is the greatest player of all time, etc, etc. He has demonstrated his lack of character in multiple ways and for me that can't be earned back. The lesson for me is to strive for consistency in my own behaviors and to be true to what I believe.

"The measure of a man's character is what he would do if he knew he never would be found out." Thomas Babington McCauley

THE END IS THE BEGINNING

Here we are. At the end of the book and the beginning of your Plan Be journey. What happens when you close the book and get back to life is up to you. The same will go for me as well because I am not just the President of the Hair Club for Men, I am a member myself.

When I teach, I always tell my students, "There is a Grand Canyon sized hole between knowing something and the ability to do it." The real work that will need to be done starts now and it comes down to you. Most people will either
a. Put the book down and go back to business as usual
b. Pick up the next self-help styled book and enjoy that flavor of the month read

And then there are those people who will do the work. I do the work every day. Sometimes I win and sometimes I lose but I do the work because I see the benefits it has reaped in my own life. The problem with motivational writers and speakers is that, much like church camp, the high wears off over time. It is easy to get fired up and be a true believer as it is happening and you are in the moment, but what do you do when you aren't feeling it? This age old question is where Plan Be gets some traction. I feel confident that this process, this language, this strategy for creating the life you have always dreamt of living, gives you the tools you need to succeed not just when you are feeling it, but when you are dragging, tired, and just plain ol' worn out.

Do the work.

Not because I need you to do it but, because you need you to do it.

Do the work.

Not because your husband, wife, kids, friends, clients, boss, neighbor, and dog need you to do it, but because you need you to do it.

Do the work.

Not because you will be skinny and rich and fabulously wonderful with a reality television show on the E! network, but because when you are living your Plan Be, you are doing the work that you were put here to do.

Do the work.

When you do the work, you inspire others to do their work. When they do their work, they inspire others to do their work.

You become a domino.

Now, get to work.

Kisses
Hugs
High Fives

*You pick, I deliver

When you undertake a project like writing a book, and then turn around and re-write that book, there are going to be some people that you must acknowledge.

Melissa Cox, my friend and book editor.

In just two years you have become one of my closest and dearest friends. Your kindness, enthusiasm, and friendship sustain me. I hope in some way I bring something to our friendship because you bring so much to my life. I adore you, and I now have a better understanding, of, when, and, where, to, use, commas.

Chad Lock, my book cover designer

Quick turn around time. That is the key to a good working relationship with a designer. Thank you for getting updates to me fast and helping me execute my vision.

Mark

You love me not only for my youthful good looks, but for my brains. I am so thankful you like smart chicks and specifically you liked this smart chick. It is so refreshing to be in a relationship with a man who values great conversation, exchanging ideas, and sees me as his equal. I work well under those conditions. Thank you.

Maddie and Trinity

You are the best thing I have ever done. The lessons I have been taught as your mother have changed me for the better. What a joy it has been watching you grow into the young ladies you are today. What amazing things are in store for your life in the years to come! I can't wait to see who you will Be when you are "all grown up".

Fini

The book is finished but the journey is not.
Growth is an ongoing process and
no matter your age you should always be
reaching for bigger and better things.
I would be honored to help you on that journey.
As an educator my passion is helping people
tap into their strengths, passions, and purpose.

Let's stay connected!

workshops | keynotes | coaching | presentation design

lspears@bravocc.com | 972.754.6023 | www.bravocc.com

Be a Bravo cc fan at www.facebook.com/bravocc

Want to share your Plan Be?

When you find your Plan Be share it with me!
I would love to see what you are doing too.
Email me at lspears@bravocc.com
and share a picture to go with your plan too!

WORKS CITED

American Student Assistance. Student Loan Debt Statistics. http://www.asa.org/policy/resources/stats/default.aspx.

Cannon, Lou. "Why Reagan was the 'Great Communicator'." *USA Today.* http://www.usatoday.com/news/opinion/editorials/2004-06-06-cannon_x.htm

Centers for Disease Control and Prevention. Obesity and Overweight, Data for the U.S. http://www.cdc.gov/nchs/fastats/overwt.htm.

Godin, Seth. "Quieting the Lizard Brain." http://sethgodin.typepad.com/seths_blog/2010/01/quieting-the-lizard-brain.html.

Hirshman, Linda. "The Truth About Elite Women." *The American Prospect.* http://www.prospect.org/cs/articles?articleId=10659.

Kelly, Tara. "80 Percent of Americans Spend an Extra Day a Week Working After Hours." *Huffington Post.* http://www.huffingtonpost.com/2012/07/03/americans-work-after-hours-extra-day-a-week_n_1644527.html.

Mandel, Michael and Steve Hamm. "The Real Reasons You're Working So Hard...and what you can do about it." *Businessweek.* http://www.businessweek.com/magazine/content/05_40/b3953601.htm.

Rowe, Mike. Learning From Dirty Jobs. http://www.ted.com/talks/mike_rowe_celebrates_dirty_jobs.html.

Schswbel, Dan. "How to use Storytelling as a Leadership Tool." Forbes. http://www.forbes.com/sites/danschawbel/2012/08/13/how-to-use-storytelling-as-a-leadership-tool/2/.

"Something Special About Southwest Airlines." *CBS Sunday Morning.* http://www.cbsnews.com/stories/2007/08/30/sunday/main3221531.shtml.

Tabaka, Maria. "Do you stink at Public Speaking?" *Inc. Magazine.* http://www.inc.com/marla-tabaka/speak-up-to-boost-your-brand-through-public-speaking.html.

Taylor, Sandie. "To Provide the Best Customer Service, Put Customers Second, Says Southwest President Colleen Barrett." *McCombs School of Business.* http://www.mccombs.utexas.edu/news/pressreleases/barrett_wrap.asp.

Tucker, Paul. *Visual CV Resume.* Feb. 6, 2010. Slideshare. http://www.slideshare.net/p4ult/paul-tuckers-visual-cv-resume-curriculum-vitae. November 2012.

Van Dusen, Allison. "Are You Taking Too Many Medications?" Forbes. http://www.forbes.com/2008/06/19/health-drugs-prescriptions-forbeslife-cx_avd_0619health.html.

Weiss, Jennifer. "Our Inane Competition over Stress Levels." *The Daily Pennsylvanian.* http://www.dailypennsylvanian.com/node/43946.

Webley, Kayla. "How the Nixon-Kennedy Debate Changed the World." *Time.* http://www.time.com/time/nation/article/0,8599,2021078,00.html#ixzz1DDt1rVLM.